A WEAVING OF WONDER

"Combines imaginative and delightful fables with wise and gentle tools for growth and illumination. A beautiful blend of enchantment, creativity, insight, and inspiration."

Louise M. Wisechild,
Author of *The Obsidian Mirror* and *The Mother I Carry*

"These beautifully written, poignant, and therapeutic journeys bring together insight and integration for some of the basic issues we face in today's world. Charlotte Brown's fables, with the wise and gentle reflections by Karolyne Rogers, allow one to appreciate the connection of past and present."

William H. Miller, Jr., M.D., Psychiatrist

"These fables are clever springboards to our spiritual selves. 'Mr. Slumpshuffle,' the kingdom of 'Talkalot,' and the 'Fidget' family encourage inner reflection while entertaining us."

Roberta Temes, Ph.D., Clinical Assistant Professor,
Department of Psychiatry, SUNY Health Science Center,
Brooklyn, New York

"Offers playful, gentle, loving guidance into your own experience and your own ways of recognizing and honoring the transitions of life."

Nancy Porter-Steele, Ph.D.,
Co-founder of Health-Based Psychotherapy

A Weaving of Wonder

*Fables to Summon Inner Wisdom
by Charlotte Rogers Brown*

*Integration Reflections
by Karolyne Smith Rogers, Ph.D.*

LuraMedia™

Copyright © 1995 LuraMedia
International Copyright Secured
Publisher's Catalog Number LM648
Printed and Bound in the United States of America

Printed on Recycled Paper

Cover image by Sara Steele.
 "One Short"
 © 1990 by Sara Steele, All Rights Reserved.
Cover design by Dan Tollas, DeStijl Corporation, Doylestown, PA

LuraMedia, Inc.
7060 Miramar Road, Suite 104
San Diego, California 92121

LIBRARY OF CONGRESS CATALOGING-IN-PUBLICATION DATA
 Brown, Charlotte Rogers, date.
  A weaving of wonder / fables to summon inner wisdom by Charlotte Rogers
 Brown : integration reflections by Karolyne Smith Rogers.
   p. cm.
  ISBN 1-880913-14-3
  1. Fables, American. 2. Self-actualization (Psychology).
 I. Rogers, Karolyne Smith, date. II. Title.
 PS3552.R68536W43   1995   95-7722
 158'.1—dc20   CIP

Permission to reprint the quotation from Jack Maguire's *Creative Storytelling* has been
graciously granted by Yellow Moon Press, P.O. Box 1316, Cambridge, MA 02238
(1-800-497-4385).

We are all weavers,
whether we know it or not.

Contents

With love and gratitude for all the "firsts" we have shared together,
I dedicate my first book to my sons, Jason and Joe.

With special thanks to . . .

my husband, Charlie, for his faith and love; to Karolyne for her
friendship and collaboration; to my parents, Eugene and Eleanor,
for being examples of strength and courage; to Andrea for the
"Dream Team"; to Darlene for believing in magic; to Mike and
Suzanne for believing in me; to "The Group" for listening; to Karin
for the joy of being her sister; to Ruth Butler for her care in editing;
and to Lura Jane Geiger and everyone at LuraMedia for all their
help and guidance.

Charlotte Rogers Brown

———

I dedicate my contribution to A Weaving of Wonder to the
memory of Robert G. Ferris, who died last summer, and to his wife,
Emar Ferris, who continues to find her unique way in the world.

I wish to thank the following . . .

Lura Jane Geiger for all her gentle guidance and wisdom in editing;
LuraMedia for the opportunity to publish; Charlotte Rogers Brown
for her delightful self and her delightful fables; the clients whom I
see as a therapist for teaching me about the process of living; my
colleagues at A Center For Human Development for their loving
support; my secretary, Barbara Dennison, for helping me manage
my time; Pam DeLeo for inviting me to explore; and Mary L.
Morris for her steadfast friendship and encouragement.

Karolyne Smith Rogers

Letters to the Reader

In his book *Creative Storytelling*, Jack Maguire writes:

> We can't expect children to deal rationally with all the pressures of growing up, which include recognizing the good and the bad in themselves as well as in others. They are well aware that life is not always pleasant; and unless this fact is acknowledged in some manner that speaks to their imaginations, they are apt to feel frustrated and insecure. Storytelling gives children more scope for working out their dreamlike perceptions of life, for symbolically confronting its myriad opportunities and difficulties. It equips them with tools—images and words—that they can use to test their intuition and powers of judgment; and it safely and gently introduces topics that can later be discussed openly outside of the privileged world of storytelling.

Read that passage again, substituting the word "adults" for "children," and therein lies a perfect description of why I write and share my fables. For just as "we can't expect children to deal rationally with all the pressures of growing up," we can hardly expect adults to always deal rationally with all the pressures of growing older.

As a child I made up stories and poems, in part as a means of making myself understood to my family and teachers, but even more for the fun of letting my imagination run free. What spilled out onto the paper would often surprise me, and that ability to surprise myself—coupled with the ability to recreate the world in any way I saw fit—thrilled and entertained me to no end.

That is, until *it* came. Until, like Carl Sandburg's fog, adulthood crept in on little cat feet, and I was transformed into wife, parent, divorcee, returning college student, newspaper reporter, lost soul. When the pain of the latter became great enough, I started writing stories again. I wrote so that I might find answers to the questions adult experience had left me, questions such as: Can I really follow my dreams? What possible good can come from being alone? What is the antidote to fear? What benefit is there to growing old?

And the answers came. Like a photographer bringing images to life in a darkroom, I watched the answers to my questions appear on my computer screen, delivered by characters of my own making. And before I knew it, I was writing again purely for the thrill of it—for the childlike joy of summoning my own wisdom.

Come, summon your wisdom, too. And as you do, I hope you will pass it on to fellow travelers, so we might all learn from each other.

From my heart,

Charlotte Rogers Brown

𝕴 am on a path to becoming a human being. On that path I encounter other travelers who appear along the way to share the wisdom of their journeys. One of those travelers is Charlotte, who one day asked me to read some stories she was writing.

At first reading, the stories delighted me with their imagination, playfulness, and use of metaphor. The second time I read them, I did so out loud, enjoying the rhythm. The third time, I began to recognize the stories of my life in them. I recognized also the stories I listen to as a psychotherapist, told to me by my clients.

"What are you going to do with these stories?" I asked Charlotte.

"I started out writing them as children's stories," she replied, "and somewhere along the way they became the stories of my own growth."

In the imagination and metaphor of these stories, I see the freedom to explore a commonness that binds us all as human beings, the commonness of the wisdom of experience made available by accessing the child-part of all of us. I picture ways of providing an opportunity to explore the uniqueness of how each of us experiences our commonality, the uniqueness reflected by the child's wisdom summoned forward to integrate the wholeness of the adult experience.

So I asked to share the wisdom of my journey with Charlotte by adding to her fables insight and integration reflections that bid other travelers to join us. These reflections are an invitation to read and hear the fables, to gather your experience of living through all your senses using the Integration Reflections as a guide, and to craft personal fables for the beginning, middle, and now of your life.

As I say regularly to myself and my clients, "You have already had the life experience. Grant yourself permission to integrate its wisdom and use it to enhance your life. What a marvelous opportunity!"

I join my heart with Charlotte's
in offering A *Weaving of Wonder*,

Karolyne Smith Rogers

Introduction

𝕵n 1964, I wrote an essay for my third-grade teacher, which my mother unearthed many, many years later while cleaning out a bedroom closet. My essay, simply titled "Future," appears here in its unedited entirety:

> *In the future I plan to be an auther. I want to write mystery books.*
>
> *In the future I may write my life story. I might draw the pictures for my books too.*
>
> *If I decide not to be an auther I might be a reporter. I would write as interesting articles as I could.*
>
> *I may be the reporter who writes down imformation about a robberie or a murder.*
>
> *I may help find a thief or maybe help find lost jewelry and things like that.*
>
> *But whatever I do I'm sure it will be exciting.*
>
>

Charlotte Rogers
January, 1964
>

No matter how many times I reread these words, I am awed by how prophetic they were—by how much I knew then about the person I am now.

I write mysteries every time I enter my thoughts and feelings in my journal or tinker with a story on my computer.

I write my life story every time I put words on a page. I often like to doodle in the margins.

I have been a newspaper reporter, working hard to make my articles as interesting and informative as I could.

I continually work at reporting events of my own life through my stories. Cloaking them in fantasy and humor, I write about false beliefs that have robbed me of joy and, at times, murdered my spirit. I reveal thieves and murderers so they cannot harm me again. I recover for myself glittering gems of inner joy, peace, and wisdom. Things like that.

But whatever I do, I find it all very exciting.

This book is about finding joy, peace, wisdom, and excitement within ourselves—anywhere and at any time in our lives. This book is an invitation to embark on a journey from adult to child and back again, many times over. As you move back and forth, you will begin to weave a pattern—one that may surprise you.

To help you get started, I offer some characters I have conjured up to lead me on my journey. I always create the main character of my fables as either a child or an adult with a child's heart and faith—someone whom I could send out into the world of story to travel on my behalf when I feel confused or "stuck." One among my vanguards is Silly Slumpshuffle, a weaver who discovers a way to weave the gnarled, twisted branches of the witchknuckle bush into wondrous baskets like none his fellow villagers have ever seen.

We are all weavers, whether we know it or not. With gentle encouragement, we can spin stories of our childhood into spools of colored thread. We can gather stories of our adulthood and do the same. Thus, finding deep within ourselves the heart and soul of an artist, we are empowered to weave our threads into works of pure wonder.

The fables contained in this book will call you back to the world of imagination and wonder, a place where the child inside you still daydreams, colors with crayons, writes boldly with big letters, moves without music, and believes in magic. In the Integration Reflections that follow each story, Karolyne offers new opportunities to reflect, color, write, and move through your life "there and then" and your life "here and now" so you can become consciously aware of how the two are magically interwoven.

Together, Karolyne and I hope this book will give you the gentle encouragement to begin spinning your thread and provide you with some tools to assist in your weaving.

The Fables

Inviting:
Before you begin reading, find a comfortable place where you will not be disturbed. Invite your inner child and your imagination to be present. Quiet your mind.

Reading:
You may wish to read the fables once silently, then once more out loud. Enjoy the sound of your voice. Try on different voices for different characters, feeling the child-part of you join in the reading.

Listening:
As you listen to yourself reading each of the fables, notice where you enter the story, where it begins speaking to you. Notice where your imagination begins making pictures of the words, when it becomes real and alive for you.

The Integration Reflections

Creating a Space:
Before beginning the reflections, create a space of relaxation and focused attention. You can use the script from the Appendix or create your own. The script invites you to clear your mind and open your spirit to receive. You may wish to make an audio tape of your own voice, using the script, or select your own words for creating a centered space.

Focusing:
Each period of reflection is initiated with a short excerpt from the fable to help you focus on a specific issue or theme.

Sharing:

Personal entries from Karolyne's journal are included to help guide you as you reflect on your life experiences. Karolyne journeys with you all the way, spinning stories of her child-self "there and then," then sharing the wisdom those stories bring to her adult-self "here and now."

Reflecting:

Insight:

The insight reflections invite you to recall experiences of your child "there and then" and your adult "here and now." Journaling, coloring, and drawing are the media offered for this reflection level. You will find tips for journaling, coloring, and drawing in the Appendix.

Integration:

The integration reflections invite you to build upon your own insight, allowing your body to teach its stories—through movement, sound, colors, nature, symbols, and celebrations—offering tools to journey from insight to integration. You will find tips for movement in the Appendix.

Personal Fables:

At the conclusion of the last integration reflection for each chapter, you are invited to create a personal fable from your own experience and to share these fables however your spirit guides. Tips for fable writing appear in the Appendix.

The fables and integration reflections are carefully designed to provide a sequential journey through adult developmental experience. Since each fable, each reflection builds upon the one before, it is helpful to proceed in the order in which they are presented.

You may easily experience these fables and integration reflections as an individual traveler, allowing yourself to move at your own pace. However, our hope is that you will invite others to laugh, cry, move, and share stories with you along the way. If you encounter memories or issues too painful or distressing to journey through alone, make your way safe by calling upon a therapist, member of the clergy, or trusted friend for assistance and support.

Our hope is that this book will open your heart to your own wisdom, which is there for the knowing, in the weaving.

A Weaving of Wonder

I

The Wooden Egg

The old man sat in the cool shade and smiled at the beauty of the forest. He took a block of wood from the pocket of his favorite coat. Out of the plain wood, he began to carve an egg.

Wooden eggs were all the old man ever carved, but each one was different. Some eggs were large, and some were small. Some eggs were white, some were brown. Some were speckled blue. Not one was perfect, but every egg was given a name, and every egg—every single one—had a special dream inside.

The old man worked on the egg all that day. It was nearly dark when he took his box of paints from the pocket of his favorite coat. He dipped his brush first into the yellow, then into the green. When the egg was finished, it was the color of spring grass. He lay the egg down on a bed of pine needles.

"Your name is Woodrow," he said. "Remember always to be patient—your dream will hatch in its own time."

The old man rested until all of the stars had come out, then he disappeared into the night.

The next morning the sun shone high above the treetops, but none of its warmth touched Woodrow in the cold damp shadows of the forest floor. He felt frightened and alone. Then he noticed a pair of eyes looking down at him from a huge circle of twigs.

"I'm Mrs. Eagle," said a voice in the branches above. "Are you lost?"

"I don't know what I am," Woodrow wanted to say, but he found that he hadn't yet a voice of his own.

"Well, no egg should be alone," said Mrs. Eagle. "And you, child, are such a bright, promising shade of green."

With that, she flew down and snatched Woodrow from his bed of pine needles. She made room for him in her nest beside her own egg who was shiny and white like a full moon.

Woodrow felt so warm and safe nestled under Mrs. Eagle's soft tummy feathers. As he lay alongside his egg sibling, he thought, 'I could be happy like this forever.' And for many days he was happy, until something earth-shaking—or rather, egg-shaking—happened.

Early one morning, Woodrow heard tapping noises coming from inside his egg sibling. Before he knew what was happening, the egg cracked wide open. In its place sat a fuzzy, wide-eyed eaglet. Mrs. Eagle named her baby "Cody."

Cody had a great deal to say right from the start.

"What's the matter with you?" she asked Woodrow. "Come on out of there, and let's play."

Suddenly, Woodrow was no longer happy. He had a terrible urge to hatch, but he remembered what the old man had said: "Be patient. Your dream will hatch in its own time."

Woodrow didn't know what his dream was supposed to be. At the moment it seemed very important to become an eagle like Cody.

"Come on," Cody encouraged. "You can do it!"

Woodrow tried with all his might, but he simply could not hatch. He could tell he was different from Cody. Worst of all, no one could see that he was crying inside. To Cody and her mother, he appeared quiet and wooden, though still a bright, promising shade of green.

As the days passed, Woodrow divided his time between practicing his patience and watching the eagle grow. Cody was so full of energy. She liked to lay on her back and wrestle Woodrow with her feet. She liked to pull her feathers down over her eyes and make funny faces. She liked to dance in the rain. Other times, Cody liked to sit back, chew on the end of a long pine needle, and talk about the future.

"When I grow up," Cody would say, "I'm going to be a real high flyer. Someday I may even fly to the moon and back. Or maybe I'll build a nest at the top of the highest mountain so that I can look out over the whole wide world."

The little eagle made Woodrow laugh inside. To Cody, of course, Woodrow still appeared quiet and wooden—though still that very bright, very promising shade of green.

No one could have been more proud or excited than Woodrow the day Cody's dreams began to come true as she attempted to fly on her own for the first time. Woodrow watched breathlessly as Cody prepared to take off.

At first Cody clung timidly to the edge of the nest. She looked up at the sky and sighed, "The moon is much too far away." Then she looked down at the ground and sighed, "I'm afraid I'd be dizzy at the top of the highest mountain."

Mrs. Eagle smiled. "Give yourself time," she told her. "Keep the moon and the mountain in the back of your mind, but for now you need only learn the simple joy of flight."

The young eagle listened to her mother. Then, as Woodrow watched, Cody opened her strong young wings and flew. Before long, Cody and Mrs. Eagle were a pair of graceful silhouettes against a deep blue sky.

Day by day, the northern breezes lifted the eagles to new heights, leaving Woodrow alone in an empty nest. By now, however, Woodrow was so patient that he wasted no time crying or feeling sorry for himself. Instead, he passed the hours doing all the things he liked best. He soaked up the warm summer sun. He delighted in the cool summer rains. He listened to the trees whisper in the wind.

Woodrow loved the trees most of all. Trees were the homes and playgrounds of all the forest creatures. 'How important and exciting that must be,' he thought. He studied the trees closely, often daydreaming about what it would be like to be a tree himself.

Then one day, something earth-shaking, *really* earth-shaking, happened.

Cody and Mrs. Eagle were somewhere off in the clouds, while Woodrow was busy enjoying himself and studying the world around him.

All of a sudden, before he knew what was happening, he rolled out of the nest onto the soft cushion of pine needles below. His bright green paint began to chip and peel, and tiny roots sprouted from underneath. The wood began to split and splinter, and from deep inside grew the branches of a fine young tree. Woodrow's tender needles were the brightest, most promising shade of green—the brightest of any tree in the entire forest.

"My dream has hatched!" Woodrow wanted to shout, and to his surprise, the words rang out loud and clear. The sound of his voice reached Cody and her mother, who flew back as quickly as they could. The three celebrated for the rest of that wonderful day.

That night, as Cody and Mrs. Eagle slept peacefully cradled in Woodrow's branches under a shimmering blanket of stars, the old man put the finishing touches on another wooden egg and smiled at the beauty of the forest.

Integration Reflections

Create a Space:

Grant yourself the gift of time by entering, leaving, and re-entering the Integration Reflections as your spirit guides you. Weave the wonder of your experience at whatever pace you need to summon and integrate your inner wisdom. Each time you re-enter the Reflections, remind yourself to create a space.

Now, get comfortable . . . take a few deep breaths . . . breathe in oxygen and quiet energy . . . breathe out whatever you do not need and let it go.

You may wish to record and play your own "Create a Space" audio tape. See the Appendix for suggestions.

PATIENCE

"Your name is Woodrow," he said. "Remember always to be patient—your dream will hatch in its own time."

THERE AND THEN: "Oh, no! There's the word 'patience' again. Now I'm not going to get what I want, when I want it. I have to be patient and wait for my brother before I eat my ice cream. Patience is what makes ice cream melt."

HERE AND NOW: "I invite patience by listening to the wind blowing through the pine trees. One fir tree at my office has a trunk so big that three people holding hands can't reach around it. I lean my head against this grandfather tree and hear the sound of patience. Patience helps me to be a better listener."

1. The patient ones were always Dad + Tim + me, Rosemary - nothing mom - guilt, I think be- cause she insisted on the vaccine - but EVERYONE did. I had to be patient. The Polio Vaccine. They were a series of 3 shots. I couldn't start my series because I had bad cold but they figured by the time R+T went for their 2nd shots I should be able to start my series which I did, BUT it turned out to be a "bad batch." To make a long story short, a yahoo (I trying to put it nicely) went into a bar named PEEC lot 49 and bragged about what he had done to a whole batch of the vaccine. The cop listeners encouraged him keep talking. Finally they pulled out their badges - he realized

what he's just done + gave himself up. He
was sentenced over 300 yrs. on
an isolated island somewhere in the
South Pacific. Well, at least we got
the answers needed.

Insight:

▶ Go back in your mind to your childhood. . . . In your journal, write about your early recollections of being patient. Allow your child-self to present memories for you.

▶ Recall the past few weeks. . . . Journal about a time when patience was present for you.
For example: being patient with a child, someone elderly, a stressed co-worker, or a friend; trying to reach a goal; waiting for something to occur.

▶ In your journal, explore your feelings and thoughts regarding patience in your life then and now.

Integration:

▶ If patience had a voice, what would it say? Say the words or message aloud to yourself. Say it several times. Call a friend and say it to him or her.

▶ Allow that message to guide you in identifying areas in your life (home, school, work, play) where patience is needed.

▶ Over the next week or so, invite patience into your life as your message guides.
For example: by praying or meditating, asking for patience from another, announcing to another your intention to be more patient, giving yourself the gift of patience, creating more time for "being."

There are some people right here in
this room who daily "try" EVERYONE'S
patience, not just mine, sometimes to
point of cruelty! That is when I know I
have to bit or my "German temper" will
explode full force — so I do spit physically,
literately. Others have "congratulated"
me on my control! That helps, really.
Apparently some one spoke up because the
"problem" is no longer allowed in this
DINING ROOM!

LOST

"I'm Mrs. Eagle," said a voice in the branches above. "Are you lost?"

"I don't know what I am," Woodrow wanted to say, but he found that he hadn't yet a voice of his own.

THERE AND THEN: "I turn around and my mother is gone. She is replaced by long rows of empty clothes hanging on racks taller than me. I wonder if the clothes got her. My feelings make me lie down and push tears out of my eyes. My throat hurts. I turn over, and I can see her legs. She reaches for me and tells me about the word 'lost,' a word for my feelings."

HERE AND NOW: "I turn around and my mother is gone. I discover that the feeling of 'lost' doesn't depend so much on someone else being or not being there. I create my own feelings of 'lost' when I try to control my life rather than allowing my life to happen. Controlling blocks avenues, direction. I can't see where I'm going. But sometimes I don't think it is cool to appear lost, so I just *look* like I know where I'm going."

Insight:

▸ Allow your mind to return to a child-time when you were lost. . . .
What were your strongest feelings? What happened that eventually
allowed you to feel at ease again? Write in your journal about a
childhood experience of being lost.

▸ Journal about a sense of being lost now.

[handwritten: I don't think I ever felt lost. I always knew I had 2 companions + Tame Dad. NEVER MOTHER OR ROSEMARY (Hm. this is the 1st time I realized Male VS Female)]

Integration:

▸ Give yourself permission to stay with the feelings of "lost." Allow
those feelings to be with you until a color seems to fit the feelings.

▸ If "lost" were a color, what color would it be? Using that color and
others that seem right, color or draw "lost" from your experiences as
a child and as an adult.

[handwritten: Lost = BLAH. color? Dirty white is the closest I can come — NO BEIGE]

▸ Spend some time with your coloring, allowing it to create a message
for you. Say the message to yourself. You may wish to journal the
wisdom of your self-message.

[handwritten: HMM — that is almost too much color & I can't draw grey or beige! But I certainly know the feeling — not as a kid but every once in while as an adult. Maybe "Baffled" more than "lost." A question of HOW COULD SHE BE SO ——? And I still encounter them today! And I still just don't understand — ?? I don't say anything unless asked. Usually all I do is give a slight shrug + questioning look. Recently that happened in a group setting, + several agreed — no words could convey the feeling / happens]

DIFFERENT

"Come on," Cody encouraged. *"You can do it!"*

Woodrow tried with all his might, but he simply could not hatch. He could tell he was different from Cody. Worst of all, no one could see that he was crying inside. To the two eagles, he appeared quiet and wooden, though still a bright, promising shade of green.

THERE AND THEN: "My shoulders slump. My chest is different from my friends'. It's flat. So I buy foam for the top of my bathing suit. When I jump in the water, the foam makes it to the surface before I do. I wonder how long I can hold my breath. Finally the lifeguard retrieves both pieces with his net. I swim underwater and pretend not to notice. The lifeguard throws 'them' away. Later, a friend tells me to use safety pins like she does."

HERE AND NOW: " 'Different' is feeling like everyone else knows what to wear. It's being single and going to a couples event. It's not speaking what I think or feel because I won't fit in. It's being pigeon-toed. I long for the time when 'different' becomes more of a celebration and less of a comparison of myself to others."

Insight:

▶ Allow your mind to wander through the years of feeling "different."
... As a child, how did you experience "different"? Write in your
journal about your feelings, your sense of "different."

I never believed I was "handicapped." But CHALLENGED — both by the polio and the deafness (95% or so). And apparently I

Integration:

▶ Allow your inner child to guide your nondominant hand in coloring
a picture of "different."

▶ Using your dominant hand, color a picture of what "different" means
to you now.

▶ Holding your pictures clearly in your mind, describe in your journal
how you feel about "different."

decided very early on — never to back down from a challenge! And, upon reflection, that is still true. If I give up — what do I have left to live for?!

POTENTIAL

His bright green paint began to chip and peel, and tiny roots sprouted from underneath. The wood began to split and splinter, and from deep inside grew the branches of a fine young tree.

THERE AND THEN: "Mrs. Brown, my third-grade teacher, writes on my report card: 'Karolyne is a delightful child to have in class, but she doesn't work up to her potential.' My mother tells me I have to start working up to my potential or I won't get the horse I want. I try harder, even though I don't know what to do. I never get the horse."

HERE AND NOW: "Potential is as freeing as 'whatever you want to be' and as binding as being told that 'girls can't be cowboys.' I know now it is a process, not an outcome. It is a daily event. I'm still not sure how to realize it exactly. Somehow that seems to be okay."

All 3 are so important in very different ways + come to mind instantly. Mary Victoria - 1st grade teacher, I used to get blinding ear aches lasting sometimes a couple weeks, out of school w head on a heating pad of some sort for some relief. It wasn't until yrs later we learned I had no eardrum in left ear to filter + that was the cause of the constant infections. I've learned to live w the aches + about 40% loss in right ear. Lip reading became a necessity - self-taught. Still useful.

so many: Sr Mary Victoria
Tim & dad
Sr Rose marine
Mrs writing

Insight:

▶ Recall a person who was important and powerful in your life as a child, maybe someone not in your immediate family. . . . Make a word picture of this person in your journal. How did this person help you discover your potential? What occurred that allowed this person to be important to you?

✗ ▶ Who most influences discovery of your potential as an adult? Journal about this influential person. *Alossar*

▶ Study your word pictures of people who have influenced your potential as a child, and now. Spend some quiet centering time with them as you read your journal.

Each of these came to mind instantly + with
a powerful "gut reaction" WoW!

Integration:

▶ Give yourself a "Realizing My Potential" celebration. After re-reading your journal entries and studying your coloring, invite "patience," "lost," and "different" to your celebration. Allow what you have learned to guide you in creating an original fable. Read it out loud, enjoying your creation. Give it the first title that comes into your mind. (There are tips for fable writing in the Appendix if you want help with crafting your first original story.)

✗ ▶ Plan your "Realizing My Potential" celebration without regard to time, money, or power. Then decide what part of the celebration you can actually do now. Invite everyone who has encouraged you to discover your potential, even if they are no longer part of your life. Celebrate with the ones who can attend. You may wish to read your first fable at your celebration.

II

The NEARLY Tragic Tale of Silly Slumpshuffle

In a little village high in the Babytooth Mountains, there once lived a basket weaver named Silly Slumpshuffle. Silly was the most successful man in the village. He had a beautiful wife, two happy children, a boy and a girl, a roomy cottage on the lake, and a prosperous shop in the village square where he sold dozens of baskets each day.

Fashioned from the twisted branches of the witchknuckle bush, Silly's baskets were unlike any the villagers had ever seen. No one but Silly had ever thought to use daisy seed oil to soften the gnarled, knotty limbs enough for weaving. As long as he alone held the secret, no one could ever hope to outsell him.

Every afternoon after a prosperous day of work, Silly walked with long, confident strides to his roomy cottage on the lake. There his children always greeted him with giggles and smiles, for Silly was the silliest father in the village. Swinging open the cottage door, he would shout, "Where are my little mushrooms hiding?"

"Under a bushel basket!" the children would answer, peeking out from under a huge basket Silly had made just for their little game. In a fit of giggles, the basket would topple and Silly would scoop up two chubby mushroom babies into his arms.

Silly's wife, Rosetta, dearly loved her young basket weaver for the imagination he put into everything—his baskets, his silly games, even the Sweet Potato Pie he cooked every night for supper. Topped with a dab of Silly's Original Sunflower Sauce, the pie made Rosetta's mouth water.

At night, while the other village children impishly bounced on their beds and refused cups of warm milk, the Slumpshuffle children snuggled eagerly under the covers to listen to one of Silly's bedtime stories. Silly wove fantastic yarns about serpents and mermaids and nearsighted ghosts who sailed upon the lake on moonlit nights. Quite often, Silly told them, the ghosts would steer their boats into the rocks, scattering their cargo of diamonds and pearls across the water. Staring out the window at the lake all aglitter, watching for ghostly vessels sailing in the shadows, the Slumpshuffle children soon fell fast asleep.

For a time Silly's life seemed so splendid, so charmed, that villagers would later scratch the hair right off their heads wondering why things began to go wrong.

Little by little, like a tire with a nail in it, Silly's life went flat. Once every villager owned a witchknuckle basket or two, business began to fall away, and the shop filled to the rafters with unwanted baskets. The occasional sale to passing tourists brought in enough money for food, though not nearly enough to pay the mortgage on the roomy cottage by the lake. So Silly was forced to move his family into the tiny apartment above his shop.

Time and opportunity seemed to drag their feet where the Slumpshuffles were concerned. Before long, the family could be seen shuffling through the streets of town, looking every bit as sluggish as their name. Every night, his shoulders slumped from lifting stacks of heavy baskets, Silly would push open the apartment door and sigh, "Where are my little mushrooms hiding?" Slumped in chairs in front of the television, the children would roll their eyes and answer, "Oh, Papa."

Silly continued to make his Sweet Potato Pie for supper every evening, but now Rosetta just picked at it. When she thought he wasn't looking, she would sneak off to the kitchen for a peanut-butter sandwich.

Without the lake to inspire him, Silly could only deliver his bedtime stories in a lifeless monotone. Many times he was the first to fall asleep.

'What went wrong?' Silly wondered. 'I do everything just as I have always done, yet I am poor and my family is unhappy.'

Thus Silly reasoned that his family must be unhappy because they were poor.

'If only I were wealthy again,' he thought. 'I would give my family all the joy and wonder money can buy.'

Then one day an umbrella salesman arrived in the village, peddling his wares door-to-door. As it happened, the first door he came to was Silly's.

"J. B. Luckenbill's the name, but most folks call me 'Lucky,' " said the salesman, a well-fed fellow dressed in a fine silk suit. "Might I interest you in a waterproof rain roof? I make them myself. No two are alike, but all are guaranteed not to leak or your money back!" He stood on Silly's doorstep, flashing a toothy smile and twirling a rainbow-colored umbrella.

"I hate to discourage you," said Silly, "but it hardly ever rains on this side of the Babytooth Mountains. The last time was nearly twenty years ago, and even then, it was hardly more than a sprinkle. I'm afraid you won't find many customers here."

"We'll see about that," said the salesman. "In the meantime, may I come in and rest awhile? My satchel has grown quite heavy."

Silly welcomed the chance to talk with another artisan. He cleared away a pile of baskets and offered Lucky a chair.

"Your baskets are exquisite, simply ex-tra-or-dee-naire," said Lucky, kissing the tips of his fingers for emphasis. Sadly, Silly admitted that he hadn't made a sale in nearly six months.

"Once we were so happy," he moaned. "But now, though I do everything just as I have always done, my baskets sit idle, my children are bored, and my dear Rosetta has lost her appetite."

"I know how to fix that," said Lucky, tapping a chubby finger against his forehead.

"So do I," interrupted Silly before Lucky could explain. "What my family needs is money—and lots of it!"

Lucky raised his eyebrows and gave Silly a sly grin. "Then perhaps I might interest you in a trade," he said.

"A trade?"

"My money in exchange for something of yours," said Lucky. Reaching into his satchel, he pulled out a sack of gold coins.

Never had Silly seen so much money in one place. "Where did this come from?" he asked.

"From selling umbrellas," said Lucky.

"And you would give it all to me?" asked Silly.

"As a *trade*," Lucky repeated.

Silly looked at the bag of shiny gold and saw the answer to all his troubles. "You can have anything but my wife and children," he said, figuring there was more than enough gold to replace everything else.

"You're sure?" asked Lucky. "Absolutely?"

"Pos-i-tute-ly!" said Silly, feeling his sense of humor returning already.

"Done!" said Lucky.

All at once, Silly felt befuddled and dizzy, as though a cloud of dust were swirling inside his head. He had to close his eyes for a moment to catch his balance. When he opened them again, Lucky was gone. Oddly enough, the shop appeared exactly as it had before. Silly concluded that Lucky must have left with some of the baskets from the rafters.

"I have so many, he could have taken a hundred or more and I would scarcely notice the difference," he said, running his fingers through Lucky's sack of gold, or rather, *his* sack of gold. "Why am I sitting here talking to myself when there is so much to do!"

Dashing out the door, Silly set out on a full-fledged, four-alarm shopping spree. At the toy store, he filled a dozen shopping bags with blocks of all colors and shapes for the children. At the kitchen shop, he bought every sort of gadget for whipping up new and tasty meals for Rosetta. His last stop was the real estate office, where he bought back the cottage on the lake. As soon as everything was in place, he sent word for Rosetta and the children to meet him at the cottage.

"Come in, come in, my little mushrooms," he shouted when they arrived.

The children's eyes opened wide before a mountain of blocks that nearly touched the ceiling. They dove eagerly into the pile, tossing wooden shapes into the air like party confetti.

"Build something, Papa," they chimed. "Build something grand!" Silly's heart swelled to have made the children so happy.

"What would you like me to build?" he asked.

"Anything you want," the children said. "Use your imagination."

For the second time that day, Silly felt strange. A thick cloud of dust whirled like a tornado inside his head. He looked at the pile of blocks. He looked at it from the front. He looked at it from the back. He looked at it from both sides. He even stood on his head and looked at it upside-down. But no matter how he looked at it, he could not imagine the blocks as anything but a formless heap.

"If you can wait a little while, I'll be happy to build something for you," said Silly, hoping the dust inside his head would soon settle. "But first, I have a surprise for your mother."

Silly took Rosetta's hand and led her to the kitchen where electric pretzel benders, automatic apple polishers, and battery-operated pizza dough tossers gleamed from every shelf.

Rosetta's mouth began to water. "My dear, clever husband," she said, clapping her hands. "Could you—would you—whip up something special for dinner?"

"What would you like?" asked Silly, thrilled to see his dear Rosetta so happy.

"Anything you want," she said. "Just use your imagination."

Suddenly Silly felt so dizzy, he had to sit down. Dust swirled so thick inside his head, he began to sneeze.

"Take your time, dear," said Rosetta. "The children and I will busy ourselves in the dining room."

Leaving Silly alone in the kitchen, Rosetta and the children set the table for the feast about to be set before them. As the sounds of grating, chopping, slicing, and stirring came pouring from the kitchen, Rosetta swallowed hard to keep her mouth from watering.

At long last, Silly burst from the kitchen. "TA DAH!"

Rosetta and the children looked at him with utter bewilderment. Grinning like he'd just won a blue ribbon at the fair, Silly presented them with . . . a Sweet Potato Pie!

One whiff of Silly's Original Sunflower Sauce and Rosetta's mouth dried up like the Mohave Desert. "Not again!" moaned the children before excusing themselves to make a peanut-butter sandwich.

Though he didn't say it, Silly felt as bewildered as anyone. Surrounded by every kitchen gadget known to modern science, he had tried with all his might to imagine some exotic new dish to make for his family. Still the only vision to rise out of the dust inside his head was the same tired old dinner he'd been making for years. He could only hope that his family wouldn't notice. But they did.

"What you need is a good night's rest," said Rosetta. "Are you feeling up to telling one of your bedtime stories?"

"Pos-i-tute-ly!" said Silly, seeing an opportunity to redeem himself. He loved dreaming up those stories as much as his family loved hearing them.

With Rosetta and the children snuggled in close beside him, Silly began, "Once upon a time . . . Once upon a time . . ."

Nothing. There was nothing in Silly's mind but that infernal cloud of dust. He felt so befuddled. All he could do was hold his head in his hands and cry.

"It's all right, Papa," said the children. "You can start over. Just use your imagination."

All at once, he knew.

"I can't," he cried. "I traded it. I traded my imagination to an umbrella salesman for a sack of gold so we could all be happy again. Now I own toys, and gadgets, and a cottage on the lake, but I don't have the slightest idea what to do with them!"

Rosetta couldn't stand to see her young basket weaver so unhappy. After Silly had cried himself to sleep, she and the children stayed up all night, packing up the building blocks, kitchen gadgets, and the deed to the cottage, and loading them into the wagon. They drove into the village where they pounded on doors and pleaded with sleepy shopkeepers to buy back their wares. The sun was just coming up when Rosetta and the children returned to the empty cottage with a sackful of gold.

Silly hardly knew what to say about that. Then again, without his imagination, he hardly knew what to say about anything.

"Go find your umbrella salesman," said Rosetta. "Find him and get your imagination back."

Silly ran all the way to the village, though he wasn't the least bit concerned about how to find Lucky. Although the streets would be crowded with villagers going about their business, a rainbow-colored umbrella would stick out like—well, like an umbrella.

So Silly was surprised, to say the least, to reach the village and see hundreds of umbrellas! In less than a day, Lucky had somehow managed to sell an umbrella to every single person in the village. Nevertheless, Silly was able to find him in an instant. Amid a sea of umbrellas, Lucky was the only person who wasn't carrying one.

"Please, Lucky," pleaded Silly. "Give me back my imagination."

"Why should I?" asked Lucky. "You weren't using it. But, as you can see, I've done pretty well with it so far."

"I'll give you back your sack of gold," said Silly. Some dust came puffing out his ears.

"Not interested," said Lucky.

Dust swirled about Silly's head, and he began to sneeze uncontrollably. He sneezed until his face looked like an overripe tomato.

"Oh, all right," said Lucky. "I've sold all my umbrellas anyway. And besides, there's never a shortage of people letting their imaginations go to waste. I can easily pick up another one somewhere down the road. Silly people like you give it up for a song."

In an instant the dust cleared from Silly's head, and, in its place, were some fabulous ideas! Ideas for new games to play with the children. Ideas for new dishes to cook for Rosetta. Ideas for new bedtime stories.

And best of all, he thought of something else besides baskets that he could make from the twisted branches of the witchknuckle bush: furniture! Soon everyone would be clamoring to buy Silly's newest creations, and his money troubles would be over. He couldn't wait to rush home and tell Rosetta—as soon as he had the answer to one last question.

"How *did* you manage to sell umbrellas in a place that never rains?" he asked.

Lucky only tapped a chubby finger against his forehead and disappeared into the crowd.

In no time at all, Silly, Rosetta, and the children were a happy family again. Silly sold furniture faster than he could make it. And when the village was saturated with witchknuckle tables and matching witchknuckle chairs, he came up with an idea for witchknuckle bird cages.

For their part, Rosetta dreamed up all sorts of new casseroles and the children frequently entertained Silly with a bedtime story.

Life was always changing at the Slumpshuffle house, and they liked it that way.

Integration Reflections

Create a Space:

Grant yourself the gift of time by entering, leaving, and re-entering the Integration Reflections as your spirit guides you. Weave the wonder of your experience at whatever pace you need to summon and integrate your inner wisdom. Each time you re-enter the Reflections, remind yourself to create a space.

Let your breath become a little deeper, a little slower . . . allow your body to breathe in its own rhythm . . . invite your mind to become quiet, to relax along with the rest of you.

You may want to listen to your "Create a Space" tape to hear your own words of centering.

IMAGINATION

Silly's wife, Rosetta, dearly loved her young basket weaver for the imagination he put into everything—his baskets, his silly games, even the Sweet Potato Pie he cooked every night for supper.

THERE AND THEN: "There are three kids I play with most weekends. We call ourselves the Sneaking Gang. On Saturday we get together and imagine things that might require sneaking to happen. This Saturday it is a herd of wild horses that needs to be sneaked up on so we can pick the ones we want to keep. I already know I want the white one."

HERE AND NOW: "My imagination is yellow and bright like the sun. It shines on me, fills my heart, and makes me taller. When I was a child, my imagination created what I wanted in my life. It still does. A wise woman said to me recently, 'Imagination is freeing yourself for what you want to do.'"

Insight:

- Allow yourself to drift back into childhood when your imagination was fully present. . . . Journal about an especially vivid memory. *For example*: a time when someone read to you or told you a story, or when you were pretending. *Goddde, hold to liden*

- Journal about a recent time when your imagination was present. *For example*: when you heard a story or saw a movie, when you needed to figure out a way to do something differently.

- Explore in your journal about your imagination from the child "then" to the adult "now." If your imagination had a voice, what message would it give? Say the message out loud. *Reality set in + had to grow up.*

Integration:

- Take your imagination for a walk and allow your imagination to select something from nature. It can be a snapshot of some thing, place, or scene that your imagination points out that you can keep in your mind, or an object you can take with you to put in a special place. *The violets that bloomed by the creek.*

- Let your child- and adult-self select a color for your imagination. You may want to picture or hold your imagination's gift from nature while you are deciding. *green — always out in nature*

- Close your eyes and breathe the color of your imagination deep into your belly. Allow the color to swirl and float until a shape takes form. Gently allow your body to move into that shape. Wrap your arms around your body-shape and give your imagination a hug.

- Invite yourself to write or color about your experience.

Also finding a patch of wild Violets by the creek, at least until 4th grade. When I could no longer walk down the lane — my world seemed to end — for awhile.

LIFE PATTERNS

*Little by little, like a tire with a nail in it, Silly's life went flat . . .
'What went wrong?' Silly wondered. 'I do everything just as I have
always done.'*

THERE AND THEN: "Whenever my mother or anyone asks what I want
for a present for any special time, I say what I always say, 'I want a horse
more than anything.' I ask for one for my birthday, Christmas,
Thanksgiving—anytime and every time anyone asks what I want. My
mother always tells me the same thing: 'You have your dog, Brownie,
and that's enough!' Every time I don't get a horse for a present, I refuse
to go to bed or to do anything I am asked until I get a horse. Most of the
time I lose my allowance, can't see my friends, and don't get to play with
Brownie."

HERE AND NOW: "I use the same confrontive communication style with
my favorite difficult person over and over. I believe that if I am not
confrontive, I won't be heard. It takes me a while to realize it is not
working. I feel frustrated and stuck. I don't know what to do."

No, that's not my style. Mother
always said, "She'll get over it"—
whatever "it" was. She always
believed whatever I did was just to
'get attention' since I was the youngest. I would give her the silent
treatment, which Dad & Time supported, and I never gave in.

Insight:

▶ Allow yourself some time to explore, in your journal, life patterns that may have been effective at one time but ultimately went "flat." *For example:* ways of interacting with a ~~favorite~~ difficult person, with friends, with your family (as a child and now), in your work. *I still find ignoring someone MOST effective.*

▶ Focus on the "flat" pattern that was most powerful as you wrote about it. Picture yourself in a situation when that pattern was present. Journal about what happened. How did you feel? What were your thoughts? Who was present? What labels and/or words best describe the pattern? *I still find ignoring the provocatives the most effective way to deal w/ her — she can't stand to be ignored + the others know I won't give in.*

Integration:

▶ Keeping the focus on the pattern you have written about, go back and read the "flat" pattern description from your journal. Select a word or label that best describes the pattern. *Refusing to acknowledge the irritant still works.*

▶ As you say the pattern word or label out loud, where in your body do you feel it? Gently place your hand on the place on your body that matches the word or label. *Turning my back or*

· *For example:* When I say the word "frustrated," my hand moves to my chest and forms a fist. *exiting the room*

▶ Close your eyes and breathe into the place your hand is touching. Allow yourself to spend time with the pattern-feeling.

▶ Invite yourself to talk or write about the experience.

It still works. Inevitably the person gets the message that I won't be provoked no matter how she tries. I always WAIT for her to give in or up, and initiate the conversation if she wants a resolution. If not, that is HER CHOICE, not mine.

QUICK FIXES

"I know how to fix that," said Lucky.

"What my family needs is money—and lots of it!" . . . Silly looked at the bag of gold and saw the answer to all his troubles.

"Done!" said Lucky.

THERE AND THEN: "I decide that if I make money selling night crawlers to my dad for fishing, and if I give the money back to my parents, they will buy me a horse. My parents put my night-crawler horse-money into a savings account for school clothes."

HERE AND NOW: "Sometimes I think if I get thinner, or work harder and buy lottery tickets to get more money, or take something to feel better, the things that aren't working in my life will be fixed."

That is not my way.

Insight:

▸ Recalling the "flat" pattern you identified, or another pattern that has power for you, journal about quick fixes you have explored for dealing with these patterns. What are/were your thoughts and feelings about quick fixes that did not work? About ones that did work?

I remember learning early on that there is no such thing. If something is bad enough to be "broken," the problem can't be fixed "quickly." Patience is med to heal or fix

Integration:

▸ Find a pillow or something else soft and pleasant. Allow the pillow or item you select to become your child- and/or adult-self experiencing thoughts and feelings of when you tried a quick fix and it did not work. Hold it gently as you protect and nurture your pillow-self.

▸ Allow your body to fill with feelings of your life going "flat" and not being able to find something to make it better. Gently allow your body to move into a shape that fits your thoughts and feelings. Reassure yourself that you can provide a safe place for yourself even when you experience the "flat" times.

▸ Give your pillow-self and your body-self a hug. Allow yourself to feel safe as your body moves out of the shape and fills with a sense of well-being.

▸ Write about your experience, perhaps from the pillow's point of view.

Nope - nothing here. Maybe later.
It's later and still nothing. much

RENEWAL

In an instant the dust cleared from Silly's head, and in its place were some fabulous ideas! . . . And best of all, he thought of something else besides baskets that he could make from the twisted branches of the witchknuckle bush: furniture!

THERE AND THEN: "I see my dog, Brownie, eating grass, so I imagine Brownie can be the horse I always wanted. Although he is not big enough for a good riding horse, he makes a very good leading horse. He stays tied up in front of houses I visit."

HERE AND NOW: "I feel frightened when I try to let go of an old pattern or a limiting belief, especially when I'm not sure what will take its place. I rely a lot on both my faith and imagination that the 'dust' will clear and a feeling of renewal and new insight will occur. Each time I experience the fear and the faith, I gain reassurance in my ability to nurture myself and feel safe as I cope with changes in life."

Insight:

▸ In your journal, write about a time when you were struggling with an old pattern and something came to you "in an instant," when "the dust cleared . . . and in its place were some fabulous ideas!" When did you know you needed to "let go" of the old pattern? What value did the experience of going through "flat" times have? How did you get to the "dust clearing" stage? How was your imagination present?

▸ Picture the "dust clearing" and describe or color what you see.

green - the color of new life and there for HOPE.
and lilacs + purple pansies!

Integration:

▸ Select an article of clothing that fits the color of your imagination. Put it on and breathe in your imagination. *I'm wearing it!*

▸ Re-read your journal entries and study your coloring for this fable. Allow all you have experienced to be present as you invite your imagination-clad self to write a personal fable about "imagination," "patterns," "quick fixes," and "renewal." Have the adult- and child-parts of you select a title for your fable. If you would like some help with your fable, review tips for fable writing in the Appendix.

▸ Share your fable with a friend and/or family member.

I don't share what comes from deep-within, easily. Never have + even tho' I've tried to figure this out I never been able to find the answers.

III
Waiting for Oompa

O n one of those cold mornings in January, when the moon lingers in the daytime sky, Alicia wrote a letter to her grandfather.

"Dear Oompa," she began. "I can hardly wait for you to come and live with us."

Alicia meant it with all her heart. Though she was only a baby the last time she saw Oompa, she could imagine what he was like from the stories her mother told. Sometimes Alicia thought she truly did remember the way her grandfather's cheeks bulged like a bullfrog when he played "oompa, oompa, oompa" on his tuba. Alicia had called him Oompa for as long as she could speak.

From stories and old photographs, Alicia drew a picture of Oompa in her mind. His hair was golden, just like hers. He had broad shoulders and strong, rough hands from working on his farm. On winter evenings, he liked to dance and to play his tuba. In the summer, he played baseball and ate ripe red apples from his orchard.

"Waiting is hard," Oompa wrote back to Alicia. "I must wait to sell my farm before I can leave. To pass the time, I tell stories to the man in the moon. You might try it. He's a wonderful listener."

'What a funny thing to say,' thought Alicia. She tried it a few times, telling the tales of Goldilocks' bears, Jack's beanstalk, and Cinderella's lost slipper.

"Those are all the stories I know," she told the moon, after she'd finished the one about a wolf and a boy named Peter. "I guess we'll both just have to wait for Oompa."

She wondered if Oompa ever ran out of stories, too.

Alicia busied herself preparing for Oompa's arrival. There was still much to do. She needed to learn some new dances. She needed to practice her curve ball. She needed to find an orchard where they could pick apples. Keeping up with Oompa would not be easy.

Alicia loved to imagine their time together: "Please, Oompa, play me another song," she would say, though he would have already played many.

"Another?" he would say with a twinkle in his eye. "I don't believe I know any more."

"Just one more. A marching song."

Then he would shake his head as though he couldn't think of a single note, hoist the tuba on one shoulder, and "oompa, oompa, oompa" some more. Notes would come marching from its shiny bell like they had feet.

Alicia imagined herself marching right along with them, twirling a silver baton.

Oompa finally arrived one day in early spring. Alicia sat anxiously at the window, watching for Oompa's car and daydreaming about all the busy afternoons to come. Her heart quickened when, at last, she heard a car rattling up the gravel drive.

"He's here! Oompa's here!" she called as she raced across the lawn to meet him. She reached out, ready to be swept into the air by two strong hands.

The car door swung open, and a grey-haired gentleman slowly eased himself out of the sedan. A coat hung loosely on his shoulders, and in one hand he gripped a wooden cane. Alicia stood wondering who this unexpected visitor could be.

The old gentleman looked at her and smiled.

"This can't possibly be Alicia," he said. "The last time I saw her, she nearly fit into the palm of my hand."

"Oompa?" Alicia whispered. He looked nothing at all like the man in the photographs, the man in her mother's stories. She took his hand and walked with him to the house where her parents were waiting.

In the days that followed, Alicia and her parents did a lot of waiting.

They waited for Oompa to come downstairs for breakfast.

"I'm an old sleepyhead this morning," he would say as he eased himself down the steps.

Then once Oompa sat down at the table, they waited for him to finish his meal.

"Ben, these pancakes are delicious," he would say to Alicia's father. "I want to enjoy every bite."

Whenever she took her dog, Columbus, for a walk, Alicia waited for Oompa to get his coat. Then with Columbus tugging impatiently on the leash, she waited for Oompa to stop and greet each neighbor along the way.

Every evening, Alicia waited to hear the "oompa, oompa, oompa" of a tuba. But Oompa's tuba stayed in his room, resting silently in the corner. Oompa played the radio instead.

Alicia's mother told her to be patient. "Oompa is getting older," she said. "He moves a little slower."

Alicia thought about her plans to dance together, to play baseball together, and to pick apples under the hot summer sun together. Oompa never did any of those things anymore. Instead he built flower boxes, tended the vegetable garden, and helped with the housekeeping. On rainy days he read or worked on jigsaw puzzles.

One night after Alicia had gone to bed, she overheard her parents talking in the next room.

"I don't know what to do, Ben," her mother said. "I'm running out of jobs for him around the house."

Her father said he wished there were more people Oompa's age in the neighborhood. He said he just didn't have as much time to spend with Oompa as he'd like.

Alicia's mother said she sometimes felt like taffy, pulled in all directions.

Alicia didn't understand what her mother meant.

In July, a man about Oompa's age came to visit the family next door. For the next two weeks, Oompa and Thomas—that was his name—spent a lot of time on the porch teasing about which was the best team in baseball. Oompa said it was the Pirates. Thomas said, "You say that only because you're from Pennsylvania. The Yankees—now there's a baseball team!" Oompa asked if Thomas's opinion had anything to do with being from Albany.

The day Thomas left, Oompa stood at the front window and waved good-bye. He stayed by the window until the car carrying Thomas to the airport drove away. Alicia thought he looked sad even as he smiled at her and said, "Thomas has to leave so that we can all feel excited again when he comes back."

Oompa looked out the window a lot. He knew exactly what time the mail carrier came by every day. If she was on schedule, he'd say, "Half past ten, right on the nose!" If she was late, he'd watch until he saw her car coming up the street. Then ambling out to the curb, he'd offer her a rose from the garden and say, "Don't let 'em work you too hard today, Doris."

Every evening Oompa watched for Alicia's father to come home from work. And even if the time grew late, Oompa wouldn't consider starting dinner without him.

"I'd rather wait," he'd say. So Alicia would wait, too, even though her stomach was growling.

One day when Alicia was sitting on the lawn holding hands with Frankie Smith, she looked up and saw Oompa waving at them. Alicia let go of Frankie's hand and wished Oompa didn't have to watch everybody so much.

But Alicia began watching Oompa, too, when she thought he wasn't looking. His pants bulged at the knees from the hours he spent at his work bench or in his chair reading. He cleaned his glasses several times a day, rubbing the lenses with a soft cloth he kept in his pocket. His fingers wouldn't straighten and his knuckles looked swollen and sore, but his glasses always came out clear as spring water.

Most everything Oompa touched looked better somehow. Since he came, the garden had more flowers, more birds came to the feeders, and more people smiled and waved as they passed by the house.

Fall arrived with its wine-colored days and frosty nights. One evening after sundown, Oompa got up from his jigsaw puzzle, opened the screen door in the kitchen, and went outside. Through the window, Alicia could see him on the porch steps, quietly watching the moon as he would a car coming up the road.

"Would you like some company?" Alicia asked as the screen door slapped shut behind her.

"Come, join us," said Oompa. "The moon and I are telling stories."

As they sat together under the moon, Oompa told Alicia stories about his life on the farm. He talked of sliding into home plate in a wheat field still prickly with stubble. He talked of gliding across the dance floor, holding his lovely bride in his arms. He talked of how the crowds cheered and waved as he marched down Main Street playing "oompa, oompa, oompa" on his tuba. He talked of the sweet taste of home-grown apples on hot summer afternoons, and the even sweeter taste of her grandmother's apple pie on a wintry night.

Oompa knew so many stories! Alicia listened to every word, and hours passed as though minutes.

As he told his stories there in the moonlight, Oompa seemed to change before Alicia's eyes. He looked just as she had imagined during all those months of waiting: a handsome farmer with golden hair and strong hands that could do anything.

"I love you, Oompa," said Alicia, as the man in the moon looked down on them and smiled.

Integration Reflections

Create a Space:

Grant yourself the gift of time by entering, leaving, and re-entering the Integration Reflections as your spirit guides you. Weave the wonder of your experience at whatever pace you need to summon and integrate your inner wisdom. Each time you re-enter the Reflections, remind yourself to create a space.

> Find a comfortable, quiet place . . . breathe in and out with the rhythm that feels natural . . . relax and let go a little more with each breath . . . let yourself go deep inside and give yourself permission to fully experience and feel whatever you need.

You may wish to play your "Create a Space" tape to more fully relax and center yourself before you begin.

FAMILY HISTORY

From stories and old photographs, Alicia drew a picture of Oompa in her mind. His hair was golden, just like hers. He had broad shoulders and strong, rough hands from working on his farm.

THERE AND THEN: "I sit with my mother when she tells me stories that are the history of my family. She is busy, so she doesn't do it very often. But when she does, I like it very much. She tells me the story of my grandfather who is a sheepherder. She tells me of times he walks up a mountain with his shovel to dig ditches for water to irrigate sheep pasture. He lives in a log house with a wood stove, and with a toilet that doesn't flush and is in a little house outside the cabin. There is a fence around his cabin and a lot of pasture and the sheep live in the yard. I picture my grandfather as tall and skinny from walking up the mountain a lot. He sleeps in long underwear and lives in a town called Castle Dale, Utah. My mother says I can go help him herd his sheep next summer."

HERE AND NOW: "I love stories of my family history. I wish my mother had spent more time sharing our oral history. I am the youngest in my family by ten years, and sometimes it seems that all the stories were told before I was born. Stories about my grandfather taught me about living close to the land. He taught me not only how to conserve the land's energy but also how to conserve my own energy by moving more slowly and more thoughtfully when I helped him with his chores. He taught me about growing old. I still cherish stories of my family and look forward to times when my brothers and I get together and conversations begin with, 'Remember when we were kids and . . .' " We never have conversations like that. Or when we do they aren't positive — at least for ME! I was always on the "wrong

Insight:

▶ Invite yourself back into child-time. . . . Recall a favorite family story of a grandparent or elderly friend. Take a few minutes to picture yourself as a child listening to the story. *Gramma & Grandpa were very ill + all in my earliest memory —*

▶ In your journal, write the story as you remember it. *Since Dad*

▶ Write about what made the story special to you. What messages did you receive about the grandparent or elderly friend regarding aging? *this was an adventure*

▶ Think of a story about your life now that you tell—or would like to tell—about your process of growing older.

▶ Journal the highlights of this story to capture the essence or mood of it. Note the messages that speak of aging. *to know about*

My RAPE occurred. It took me a long time to be able to name it for what it was. And I still have a physical reaction when I encounter ... found out what happened, Tim's friend was arrested for some kind of rape, send a juvenile "prison" and my Dad lost valued friends. However they did ...

Integration:

▶ Re-read a favorite childhood story about a grandparent or elderly friend. Invite your child-mind to color a "mind picture" of the story picturing how the elderly friend looks. *Where M+D found out*

▶ Ask the child-part of you to join your adult-self in coloring that "mind picture" on paper.

▶ Study your coloring for a moment and allow the person in the picture to speak to you about aging. What words would she or he say? Say the words out loud to yourself. Write the words on your coloring. *understand English/ things*

▶ Grant yourself permission to invite a friend and/or family member to enjoy your stories about aging from childhood and now. You may choose to read your favorite childhood story out loud or have it read to you. Share your coloring and/or read aloud the story of your adult experience with the aging process. *When Gramma Springer came to stay w us for 3 mo, we were told she was "hard of hearing" so we were very patient w her. That wasn't true, she did understand English. Somehow I was the one to discover this. Dad a friend who*

STRUGGLES OF AGING

"I don't know what to do, Ben," her mother said. "I'm running out of jobs for him around the house" . . . Alicia's mother said she sometimes felt like taffy, pulled in all directions.

THERE AND THEN: "I see 'old' when I look into my grandfather's face. His body shows me what it looks like to get old. I see him struggle to get up from a chair. My mother says when you get old like my grandfather, you have to live with people who can help take care of you, and sometimes you die. I ask my grandfather if what my mother says is true. He says it is and tells me he will come to live with us because he is very sick. He also tells me not to be afraid when he dies. I tell him that I have never known anyone who died and that I won't be afraid." *On a farm you learn to live death + new life* LAMB

HERE AND NOW: "When I look into the mirror, I notice I look like my mother but that I never acquired her beautiful gray hair. I have met many people since my grandfather who have died, and I still haven't been afraid. I have cared for elderly friends when they were in need. I am concerned about how elderly people are cared for and about becoming dependent for my own care as I age. Some of my friends share with me their struggles about taking care of their elderly parents."

*** *I'm already in a wheelchair but that has nothing to do w aging, my hearing als has nothing to do w aging as many people's seem to. Sometimes things just wear out with age. Whether objects or senses or bodies*

Insight:

▶ Invite yourself to take a few minutes and locate a photograph or two of yourself as a child. If you do not have any on hand, close your eyes and allow the child-part of you to present you with a "mind picture" of yourself as a child. Journal your feeling as you look at, or picture, the "child" you. What did "old" mean to you then? *Frail grand-parents who needed help, But that was OK to me.*

▶ If you have a recent picture of yourself, look at it for a minute or two. You may also wish to use a mirror, or close your eyes and picture how your face and body look. Do not rush. Take time to look at yourself. Write about the experience of spending time "looking" at yourself. What do you "see" regarding growing older? What, if any, are the "struggles?"

▶ Journal about the possibility of becoming more dependent as you age.

▶ Write your thoughts and feelings about being a caretaker for an elderly friend or family member. *I think, as an AOP, our circumstances are very different, for me the altimers is the one factor that is presenting itself. But I know I'll be taken*

Integration:

▶ Contact one or more of your favorite elderly people and invite them to share their thoughts and feelings about aging. Invite your inner child to color or draw pictures of what you hear.

▶ Go to a still place inside yourself, recalling the words you heard and remembering your coloring. As you can, share your experience with friends, family, or a favorite elderly person.

care of, so I am not afraid. One of the benefits of community. We always took care of gramma, so I saw "aging" first hand, so that makes it less scary for me. I feel sorry for those who didn't grow up w grandparents. Multi-generations together are a Good experience! a natural environment. And wisdom is gained w age + experiences (why don't I feel "wise?")

GIFTS OF AGING

Most everything Oompa touched looked better somehow . . . the garden had more flowers, more birds came to the feeders, and more people smiled and waved as they passed by the house.

THERE AND THEN: "My legs are finally long enough to reach the pedals on my bicycle. My brother holds me up, lets me fall, then finally I can do it on my own. I am old enough to ride!"

HERE AND NOW: "The gifts of aging in my life are measured by all the 'firsts': the first time I could write my name, the first time I could read words in a book, the first time I rode a bicycle, the first time I won a competition, the first time I went hunting with my father, the first time I fell in love, the first time I felt I had something to say, the first client I saw as a therapist, the first time I felt the joy of bringing a dream/vision to reality, the first time I discovered I had power to orchestrate my life in a way that was right for me, the first time I discovered a difference between religion and spirituality, the first time I realized I no longer needed to try to control my life, the first time I recognized the wisdom that comes from the experience of aging."

Insight:

▶ In your journal, write a thank-you letter to "aging" for all the gifts you have received. Take time to explore the wisdoms, learnings, and changes. *I think there is a difference between aging and getting older. When many things get older, they get stale or loose flavor. I know some foods, like cheese, are aged, or wines are aged in certain*

Integration:

▶ Invite yourself to a party to present the "gifts" of aging to yourself. You may want to read your thank-you letter out loud.

▶ Read over your journal entries for this fable and allow the child-part of you and your adult-self to create a personal fable about aging. You can narrate your story with some or all of your journal entries and colorings regarding your "history," "struggles," and "gifts" of aging. Then read your fable out loud to yourself and give it a title. For additional tips on fable writing, see the Appendix.

▶ Invite friends or family to exchange aging "history," "gifts," and "struggles." Share your fable with them.

types of barrels intentionally. As for people, WISDOM comes w/ age + experience. Unfortunely far too many concentrate on the struggles and don't even believe there are any blessings. Like what can only be learned thru experiences, even those seemed only negative at the time, like with Tim and "suffered the consequences." P. O'S would never accept responsibility+.. was banned from all contact w/ Tim, even on playground. HIS parents were responsible for hiring supervisors outside of classroom. +P. O'Sullivan, Tim acknowledged his part

IV

Jarviss Fidget and the Tower of Sand

arviss Fidget was awakened from a wonderful dream by a painful pinch on her big toe.

"Ouch! That hurts!" squealed Jarviss, opening her eyes and reaching for the small kerosene lamp beside her bed. Still groggy from sleep, she looked at her foot to find a rather large crab dangling from her toe.

Living in their cave on a remote island in the Pacific, Jarviss and her family often suffered such rude awakenings because of their habit of sleeping with one foot on the ground. Should a hurricane, tidal wave, earthquake, or some other unexpected disaster occur during the night, the Fidgets wanted a head start in dashing for the open beach. Generations of Fidgets had lived by the motto, "Worry first, then prepare for the worst."

Giving her foot a firm shake, Jarviss sent the crab hurtling toward the mouth of the cave, over the long row of beds where the other members of her family slept. The crab landed with a "thud" beside Grandpa Nic's bed, then scurried out of the cave . . . but not before giving Grandpa Nic's toe a good hard pinch.

"What's happening? What's wrong? An earthquake? A tidal wave?" shouted Grandpa Nic, springing to his feet. To protect himself from falling rocks, he grabbed the helmet he kept hanging on his bedpost and plunked it on his head.

"Nothing's wrong, Grandpa," Jarviss said softly, trying not to wake the others. "It was only a crab."

Grandpa Nic grumbled something about "miserable, mean-spirited creatures" and climbed back into bed. Barely a minute had passed before he settled into a fitful sleep, punctuated by snorts, sniffles, and snores.

Meanwhile the other sleeping Fidgets were engaged in fretful conversation.

"Don't go out without your overcoat. You'll catch your death of cold," mumbled Aunt Rue, pulling the covers up close to her chin.

"I'll never, never finish all this work on time," Uncle Ar answered. His bare foot tapped an anxious rhythm on the floor while Jarviss's mother, father, and Grandma Laise joined in a chorus of "Oh dear! Oh dear! Oh dear!"

Jarviss lay awake, listening to the ocean's sure steady breath, trying to remember the dream the crab had so rudely interrupted. By the time the first light of morning reached into the cave and awakened her family, Jarviss had recaptured every dreamy detail.

She couldn't wait to tell the family about it at breakfast.

"I had the most amazing dream last night," she said as her mother dished up a plate of seaweed muffins, lightly buttered.

"You should never talk about nightmares while you're eating, dear," said Aunt Rue. "It's bad for the digestion."

"But it wasn't a nightmare," said Jarviss. "It was a real dream. You know, a good dream."

Everyone stopped eating and looked up at Jarviss. No, they did not know. A good dream was rare for the Fidgets, given the many things they had to worry about. Over the years, their faces had become lined with wrinkles and furrows. By now, Grandpa Nic and Grandma Laise had some on their foreheads that were nearly deep enough to plant corn.

"I dreamed about an enormous tower of sand," Jarviss continued. "We built the tower ourselves. All of us, together. It stood so high we could snatch the stars right out of the sky."

All the Fidgets listened with intense interest. You see, in addition to all their worries, the Fidgets shared something else: a talent for building sand castles. At every opportunity, they walked from their rocky cave to one of the island's sandy beaches. They dipped their stubby fingers into the cool, wet sand. They shaped it into walls and towers. When they were finished, castles of every shape and size sparkled brilliantly in the sun.

No one had ever matched the Fidgets' flair for fortresses.

"A tower of sand reaching all the way to the stars! That is quite a dream, sweetheart," said Jarviss's father.

"I think we should do it," said Jarviss.

"Do what?" asked Aunt Rue, nervously picking at her fingernails.

"Build a tower!" Jarviss said, her voice shaking with excitement at the very notion.

"We could never, never do a thing like that," said Uncle Ar. "Building a tower that tall is far too big a job. And besides, I don't think it's possible."

Uncle Ar stood up from his chair and, as was his custom, began pacing back and forth. Over the years, he had worn a rut knee-deep in the rocky floor.

"A tower to the stars . . ." said Grandpa Nic, with a daydreamy look in his eyes. For just a moment Jarviss thought she saw her grandfather's furrowed face begin to relax and the beginning of a smile. Then just as quickly, every furrow and wrinkle grew deeper than ever before.

"I *know* we can do it if we all work together," Jarviss insisted.

"Honey, I know you're too young to know any better, but chasing after a dream like this is much, much too dangerous," said Jarviss's mother.

Grandma Laise began tapping her fingers nervously on the table. "What if we get the thing half built, and a tidal wave comes along? What becomes of us then? Did you ever think of that?"

"What if it rains, and we all catch our deaths of cold?" said Aunt Rue, still picking at her fingernails.

"What if the neighbors see it and laugh us right into next Sunday?" said Jarviss's father. As was his custom, he began cracking his knuckles which, over the years, had grown to the size of golf balls.

"None of those things happened in my dream," said Jarviss. "We all made it to the top and filled our pockets with stars."

"Enough of this talk, or I'll send you to bed!" said Jarviss's mother.

The cave grew very quiet while the Fidgets sat around the table and, well, fidgeted. The only sounds were the cracking of knuckles and the steady tap, tap, tap of Grandma Laise's fingers.

As Jarviss sat and listened, a plan came together in her mind. As soon as she finished her muffins, she would leave the table without a word and go rummage underneath her bed for her digging tools. Then she would head for the door, banging her pail and shovel together so her family would be sure to notice. They would wonder if she might try to build the tower all by herself. Then they would begin to worry. They would worry about being left out. They would worry that Jarviss's day might be more exciting, more fun, more fruitful than theirs.

Of course, they could simply forbid her to try. But Jarviss knew they wouldn't. Because then they would worry she might become angry and rebellious. She might even grow up to be a criminal and spend the rest of her life in jail.

And so, by midmorning the entire Fidget family was on hands and knees, scooping handfuls of sand into buckets. Work on the tower was slow. The job required tons of sand to construct a base big enough to support a structure that would eventually reach stars twinkling some thirty-odd light years away.

"How long do you suppose it will take us to finish the tower?" asked Grandma Laise, who already had begun to worry she might not live long enough to see it.

"I don't see how we'll *ever* finish," whined Uncle Ar.

Nevertheless, as the day wore on, a great spiral column slowly rose up from the beach. In the waning light of evening, the Fidgets gathered up their pails and shovels and headed home for supper. Every few steps, Jarviss looked back over her shoulder at the tower's masterfully formed foundation, silhouetted against a crimson sunset.

The Fidgets got very little sleep that night. Their bodies tossed and turned amid a tempest of worries—worries of storms and tidal waves, sickness and injury, failure and ridicule.

Jarviss, too, drifted in and out of sleep, though her thoughts never left the tower. When she awoke the next morning, there were stars in her eyes.

Days passed and the Fidgets' work on the tower progressed without interruption. Nature provided warm, sunny weather, and the neighbors cooperated by staying away. This time of year, everyone was busy gathering shells and making jewelry to sell to passing cruise ships.

Then one day a solitary shell gatherer happened upon the stretch of beach where the Fidgets worked. From the corner of his eye, Jarviss's father saw the little man run across the sand and disappear among the palm trees.

"He's gone to tell everyone what we're doing," he moaned. "We'll be the laughing stock of the island."

And sure enough, the man soon returned with at least a dozen other islanders. They gathered near the base of the tower, talking and gesturing among themselves. Jarviss's father felt sure he heard the words "old," "foolish," and "stupid." Sick with worry, he cracked his knuckles until they were the size and color of ripe crab apples.

"Go on without me," he told his family as he made his way down the spiral stairway. He walked through the crowd of onlookers, dreading the sound of their laughter.

But the laughter never came. Instead, he heard his neighbors call him "bold," "fearless," and "super."

Jarviss's father fell to his knees and began to cry. Watching his family hard at work on the tower, he wanted very much to be with them all again. But his worry had sapped so much of his energy, he hadn't enough strength left to make the climb.

He spent the next several weeks in bed.

Hour after hour, hauling bucket after bucket of sand, the Fidgets trekked up and down the winding stairway. As the tower neared the clouds, Jarviss could feel the air grow cool and misty.

Aunt Rue felt it, too. "I think I'm catching cold," she said, pulling her collar up under her chin. Before long, her chest began to tighten, and she developed a hacking cough.

Worried she might die, she hurried down the tower without stopping to explain herself to the others. She ran straight home where she spent the next two months in bed with a hot-water bottle.

Jarviss, however, was having the time of her life. Perched atop the tower, she could see several neighboring islands sparkling like emeralds on a blue satin dress.

"Aren't they beautiful?" she said, pointing to the islands.

"Beautiful?!" said Grandma Laise. "They're terrifying! Absolutely terrifying!"

Jarviss wondered how her grandmother could take such a dim view of such a lovely sight.

But Grandma Laise wasn't talking about the islands. She hadn't even noticed them. All she could see were some big, black storm clouds gathering in the distance. She imagined the storm coming closer and closer, crashing in on them with the force of a thousand tidal waves.

When at last Jarviss turned to speak to her, Grandma Laise was gone. Jarviss caught only a glimpse of her silver hair as she hurried toward solid ground shouting, "Run for your lives!"

Worried she might slip and fall, Grandpa Nic followed Grandma Laise home and tucked her safely in bed.

When it finally arrived, the storm put on quite a show for the better part of an hour. It rumbled. It roared. It pierced the sky (and Uncle Ar's faint heart) with great jagged spears of lightning. Torrents of rain fell into the windswept ocean.

But the storm never reached the tower. Closing its performance with a loud clap of thunder, it departed for a previously scheduled appearance off the coast of Hawaii.

Only Jarviss, her mother, and Uncle Ar remained to see the dream through to the end. Nevertheless, the tower progressed on schedule. They doubled their efforts until they were doing the work of the entire Fidget family put together. Jarviss and Uncle Ar worked atop the tower while Jarviss's mother sent buckets of sand up on a pulley.

Growing weary from weeks of back-breaking effort, Uncle Ar became somewhat careless in his work. He didn't pack the sand quite as tightly. He even let some of it spill over the sides of the tower where it rained down on Jarviss's mother.

Then all at once an entire section of the tower gave way, sending Uncle Ar tumbling to the beach.

"I told you so! I told you this was an impossible job!" he shouted, brushing sand from the seat of his pants. "We should never have listened to such nonsense."

Then with a loud "harrummph!" he turned on his heels and trudged off toward home.

The tower was nearly finished. Just a few more steps and Jarviss would be living her dream. Jarviss sent a note down to her mother, alerting her that triumph was close at hand.

Far below, Jarviss's mother fished the note from the bucket and read it. She stood still, nearly frozen with worry—worry that they might actually succeed in building the tower after all. From such heights, she reasoned, there would be no place left to go in life but down. There would be nothing to look forward to. Nothing left to hope for. Nothing left to dream.

She called to Jarviss that she was sorry she had to go. Her words drifted away like a sea gull's cry in the wind.

As the hours passed, Jarviss had to face the fact that her mother was gone. It was then that Jarviss discovered a worry she never even knew she had, a worry about being left completely alone. Only moments ago she had felt like Jarviss the Tower Builder, Jarviss the Dream Seeker, Jarviss the Bravest Fidget of Them All. But now, suspended between earth and sky, Jarviss imagined herself the loneliest creature in the universe.

With thoughts of her family and her cozy feather bed, she took a step down the stairway toward home.

"Where do you think you're going?"

Jarviss turned around, but no one was there.

"Now I'm hearing things," she said, and took another step down the tower.

"I said, 'Where do you think you're going?' " came the voice.

"Where are you?" said Jarviss. "Show yourself."

"Finish the tower, and I will," said the voice.

Jarviss sat on the step and pondered what to do. Her cave, her family, her bed—these things were real and awaiting her return. This voice, on the other hand, might be nothing more than a symptom of too little sleep.

Then Jarviss did something no Fidget before her had ever done.

She took a chance. And before she knew it, she stood basking in the light of the most famous star in the sky, the North Star.

"Welcome," said the voice.

Out from the center of the North Star flew the most beautiful creature Jarviss had ever seen. The creature's eyes sparkled like pink ice, and her skin was the color of polished copper. Fluttering like a butterfly on lavender wings, she lighted beside Jarviss atop the majestic tower.

"Who are you?" asked Jarviss.

"I am Joy," she answered. "I never doubted you for a moment."

Integration Reflections

Create a Space:

Grant yourself the gift of time by entering, leaving and re-entering the Integration Reflections as your spirit guides you. Weave the wonder of your experience at whatever pace you need to summon and integrate your inner wisdom. Each time you re-enter the Reflections, remind yourself to create a space.

> Sit quietly and breathe . . . breathe especially into your heart, giving yourself permission again to feel and acknowledge whatever may need attending . . . simply allow the breath to do the work for you, supporting and holding you, containing the process for you.

Play your own "Create a Space" tape if you wish.

DREAMS

"I dreamed about an enormous tower of sand," Jarviss continued. "We built the tower ourselves. All of us, together. It stood so high we could snatch the stars right out of the sky."

THERE AND THEN: "I have four kinds of dreams. The sleeping kind are really neat because they don't have any rules. The awake kind are when I am someplace I don't like very much, and in my head I dream I'm someplace else. There are dreams where I think about something I want to do, that I am not doing, like riding my horse. And there are dreams I can't tell anyone about or they won't come true, like when I blow out candles on my birthday cake and wish something."

HERE AND NOW: "Each morning I wake up early, grab a towel, open the slider to the deck, and stumble outside to get in the hot tub. As the warm water soaks away the stiffness of sleep, I invite my dreams and wishes to set the stage for what I will do today. I start each morning in the hot tub, inviting my dreams and wishes to guide me. I am an early riser, so I make a wish for peace on the stars of the big dipper as it moves across the sky, honoring the passing of the seasons and the mornings of my life."

Insight:

▶ Allow your mind and spirit to focus on dreams and wishes you have in your life, ones you have had both awake and asleep.

▶ Journal about your dreams and wishes.
For example: day dreams, wishes on a birthday cake, dreams about direction in your life, dreams about things you want to accomplish.

Integration:

▶ Draw and illustrate a "Dream and Wish Map" that traces pathways of your dreams and wishes from childhood to now. Take your time. Select appropriate materials to help you: a large sheet of paper, glitter, glue, magazine pictures and newsprint words, magic markers, etc. You might want to illustrate a dream/wish at each of your life stages or at five-year intervals.
For example: At the place on the map for age five, I draw a picture of a cowboy who looks like the Cisco Kid. For age ten, I paste magazine pictures of all the horses I will have. For fifteen, I cut out magazine words, write labels, and collect pictures to paste into a classroom scene where I am the teacher. For twenty, I draw all the toys I want to buy my son. For twenty-five, I paste a picture of a college graduate and wonder if my face will ever be in that "picture."

▶ Study your "Dream and Wish Map," noticing when your dreams and wishes began to shape your life. Select one special dream or wish that stands out in your experience and set it aside to work with later.

LIMITS

[handwritten: most of these "insights" are meaningless to me.]

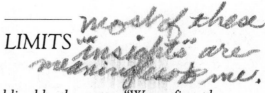

Generations of Fidgets had lived by the motto, "Worry first, then prepare for the worst" . . .

"What if it rains, and we all catch our deaths of cold?" said Aunt Rue . . .

"What if the neighbors see it and laugh us right into next Sunday?" said Jarviss's father.

THERE AND THEN: "I'm with the Sneaking Gang, and Kelly tells us a dream he had about a neat place to meet where nobody can see what we are doing. We decide to dig a fort in the vacant lot so we can go underground when we need to make sneaking plans. We start digging and get a really neat hole that is just right for all of us to sit in. We do a Sneaking Gang 'sneak' around the neighborhood to get boards to pile dirt on for the roof. My mother says, 'You will suffocate under there.' My brother says, 'That is a really dumb idea.' We cover up the roof with dirt and dig a way to crawl in and out."

HERE AND NOW: "Since being with my grandfather as a child, I dream of living close to the land, in the woods, with no neighbors, in a place where I can see deer, bear, and other animals living naturally. I find a place with forty acres next to National Forest Service land that can't be developed. The nearest neighbor is about three miles away. My banker says, 'We can't loan money on a place that is only heated with wood, that doesn't have dependable electricity, and where water is available only four months of the year.' My boss says, 'You can't live in a place where the roads aren't plowed in the winter. You won't make it to work.' My mother says, 'You can't live out there alone.' My brother says, 'Be practical. It's a dumb idea.' "

Insight:

▶ Study your "Dream and Wish Map." *always to be a teacher*

✳ ▶ In your journal, write about external limits you have experienced that
appear to block the realization of your dreams or wishes.
For example: money, what others say, health. → *it has never a*
stopped me — hearing or polio. If anything
Integration: *both have taught me patience +*
compassion

▶ Allow yourself to focus on a dream- or wish-blocking limit that has
power for you. What color is it? What sound or voice does it have?
What feelings or thoughts surround it? What power does it have to *the*
influence your dreams or wishes? *I refuse to focus on the*
negative = Blocks not helpful.

▶ Grant yourself permission to give form to your selected limit.
For example: color your limit, allow it to move you, give it voice.

▶ Notice the place in your body that responds when your dream/
wish-blocking limit is present. Place your hand on that body place and
breathe in calm and well-being.

▶ Journal about your experience with your dream/wish-blocking limit.

▶ Select something from nature or elsewhere that represents your
experience of being with your dream/wish-blocking limit. *??*

✳ External limits : hearing-loss, polio
Being a teacher takes many different forms
— w/ individuals or small groups. Also
subject matter varies. But I have
found that the definition of the term
"teacher" is broad and boundless. It
is not what I do, but who I am +
try to continue to be.

SELF-DOUBT

It was then that Jarviss discovered a worry she never even knew she had, a worry of being left completely alone. Only moments ago she had felt like Jarviss the Tower Builder, Jarviss the Dream Seeker, Jarviss the Bravest Fidget of Them All. But now, suspended between earth and sky, Jarviss imagined herself the loneliest creature in the universe . . . She took a step down the stairway.

THERE AND THEN: "What if we do finish it? What if we can't breathe enough air under there? Everybody will want to use it. We probably will get kicked out of it by the bigger kids. My brother was right, it is a dumb idea."

HERE AND NOW: "I know I won't be able to get the money for the mountain property because I really don't deserve a place like that. I'm not old enough, I haven't worked hard enough for it. My boss will probably fire me. I'll be too scared out there alone. I guess I'm just not ready for it."

When "self-doubt" I see it as un-healthy & therefore do my best not to participate.

Insight:

▶ Study your "Dream and Wish Map" and select a place where self-doubt began to interfere with your dream. Invite your dream/wish-blocking limit to join your self-doubt.

▶ Journal about similarities and differences between self-doubt and outside limits. How do they work together? Are the feelings the same or different? Which has more dream/wish-blocking power for you?

Integration:

▶ Interview your self-doubt. Make an audio tape of the conversation if possible. To set up the interview, you may wish to draw and/or picture in your mind the form and color of your self-doubt. Place that "picture," or some other representation of your self-doubt, in a chair or another place where you can see and talk to it.

▶ Ask your self-doubt to answer some questions about itself. "Self-doubt, where did you come from? When did you first show up in my life? How have you affected my ability to dream?"

▶ Select one or more key words from what your self-doubt had to say in the interview. Write them in your journal, say them out loud to the room, feel the power in them.

▶ Invite the symbol you selected for your dream/wish-blocking limit and the key words from your self-doubt interview to join you in a get-acquainted gathering. You may wish to have a conversation with them to say you honor their presence in your life. Remind them that they are only part of the process of realizing your dreams; they cannot run the whole show.

JOY

"I am Joy," she answered. "I never doubted you for a moment."

THERE AND THEN: "We use the underground sneaking fort only once. Kelly and Linda are afraid of the dark, and spiders like it too much. 'We are super, you know,' I say to the Sneaking Gang. 'If we can build an underground fort, we can do anything!' I sit with my friends and have a feeling of being together and doing something neat. I like the feeling inside me. It makes me smile and sit closer to my friends."

HERE AND NOW: "I lived on the mountain land for fifteen years. I experienced the joy of being in nature. I experienced the challenges of carrying water, felling trees, splitting firewood, growing my own food, and skiing in and out to the maintained roads in the wintertime. I grew enough food in the garden to share with the deer and elk. I repaired the side of the house after a black bear got stuck in the dog door, trying to get to the garbage cans. I did a lot of healing there. Being on the mountain is my most significant dream experience so far."

For me the "mtn" was always nature in its many forms. Even when I can't be out in nature, if I can see it, that's enough for me, summer or winter, spring or autumn.

Insight:

▶ Invite your dream/wish-blocking limit and your self-doubt to sit next to you. Thank them for helping you gain strength in realizing your dreams.

▶ In your journal, write a list of strengths you identified in your thank-you conversation.
For example: listening to myself, feeling independent, knowing the joy of accomplishment. *Being able to sit quietly + be content,*

Integration:

▶ Gather drawing materials and paper suitable for crafting a thank-you card to your dreams, limits, doubts, and joy.
For example: You may wish to draw or color a picture of joy on the front. Inside, the card might read, "Thank you, dream/wish-blocking limit, for helping me learn that what others say cannot stop me from realizing my dreams and wishes." "Thank you, self-doubt, for teaching me independence." "Thank you, God, for the gift of dreaming." You may wish to include a copy of your "Dream and Wish Map."

▶ Share your thank-you card with friends or family.
For example: Send a copy in your Christmas mailing or to someone for their birthday. Send one to yourself periodically just for the joy of it.

▶ Invite yourself to arrange and write the beginning, middle, and now of a personal fable. Ask your dreams, limits, doubts, and joys to be present to guide you as you write.

▶ Read your fable out loud to yourself, enjoying the message of your reflections. Give your fable a title and share it with others if it feels right.

V
Talkalot

There once lived a King and Queen who ruled over a kingdom known as "Talkalot." Fightalot would have been more like it, given the way the King and Queen shouted insults at each other day and night. "You addlebrained throne jockey!" was a favorite of the Queen's, while the King was especially fond of "Your mother wears chain mail."

Because their loyal subjects tended to model themselves after the Royal Family, Talkalot became known far and wide as a very noisy place.

The day Princess Winifryd was born, her parents hurled insults all the way into the delivery room.

"You're the only king in the world who wears a square crown!" shouted the Queen.

"And you're the only queen who eats lemons to sweeten her disposition!" the King retorted.

"You're three inches short of a ruler," the Queen jabbed.

"Go take a long walk on a short drawbridge," snapped the King.

"ENOUGH! BOTH OF YOU!"

The King and Queen fell silent. They were shocked—though not nearly as shocked as the Royal Physician who couldn't believe he'd spoken to his own sovereign rulers that way.

"Excuse me, but . . . It's just that . . . Well, I can't imagine this is any way for an heir to the throne to come into the world, not with all that shouting going on."

The King and Queen looked at each other. It was the first time each had seen the other's face in three years.

"I don't suppose that would be such a pleasant experience. For the baby, I mean," said the Queen. Sensing the future prince or princess was only seconds away from making a royal entrance, she screamed:

> *I hereby decree,*
> *from this day to eternity,*
> *the King and Queen shall quite agree,*
> *never again to disagree.*
> *Ahhheeeeeee!*

And with that, the Princess was born.

The King, who wanted nothing but the best for his newborn daughter, was surprised to discover he shared the Queen's opinion on this point. Still never one to be out-decreed, the King issued one of his own:

> *And I hereby declare,*
> *on behalf of my heir,*
> *no one in our kingdom fair,*
> *can utter a word of anger there.*
> *By George, it's a girl! With red hair!*

The King and Queen thanked the Royal Physician for sharing his feelings, then promptly banished him for having raised his voice to them.

The word soon spread across the land that anger was no longer permissible among the subjects under any circumstances. The palace recalled every edition of the Royal Dictionary so that the very word "anger" could be stricken from the language. As long as they were on retainer, the Royal Scribes also did away with "exasperation," "irritation," "frustration," "annoyance," "dander," and numerous other words.

The King and Queen would have been wise to do something about the word "indigestion" when they had the chance. For no sooner had they placed the official seal upon their edict, than their majesties' stomachs began to rumble. The King emitted a series of short burps, while his Queen lost her tea and crumpets in a most un-regal fashion. Unfortunately, the duties of tending to Princess Winifryd left no time to address anything so mundane as a little flatulence.

Meanwhile, the citizens of Talkalot did their best to abide by the new law. One morning a peach peddler named Mary came to the corner on which she had been selling her wares all summer long—only to discover an apple peddler named David had taken her place.

Assuming she was the victim of a premeditated takeover, Mary seethed with anger. Forbidden by law to say so, however, she was forced to take more drastic action.

"EEYOW!" howled David, wincing and jumping up and down. "You just rolled your cart over my toe!"

"Did I? I'm ever so sorry," said Mary, as her cart continued its journey over the competition's other foot.

The injured peddler stumbled, overturning his cart and sending into the street dozens upon dozens of apples—many of which were immediately squashed by a team of Clydesdales on their way to a local brewery.

David rose to his feet and was just about to unleash a host of illegal sentiments when he glimpsed a familiar uniform from the corner of his eye. Anticipating a 285A—the Royal Law Enforcement Code for "anger in progress"—a constable who had witnessed the entire incident approached the peddlers with handcuffs at the ready. Inspired by the prospect of doing time in a dungeon, the peddlers smiled at each other and shook hands, whereupon Mary let out an enormous belch. David's stomach answered with a growl so loud it startled a German shepherd napping in a nearby doorway.

Satisfied, though somewhat repulsed, the constable merely asked the pair to clean up the cobblestones, then issued each a citation for polluting the air.

Meanwhile, another potentially litigious encounter was brewing in a field beyond the village. Prompted by a particularly bad case of indigestion—brought on by the incessant barking of his neighbor's dogs—a farmer named Alphonse walked to his toolshed, took out a scythe, and proceeded to shear the sunny heads off his neighbor's marigolds.

"Hey!" shouted his neighbor, Peter, who happened to glance out the window in time to see Alphonse start on the hollyhocks. He grabbed the outlawed edition of the dictionary he kept hidden behind the encyclopedia and ran outside, fully armed with a complete, uncensored listing of expletives.

No doubt a serious confrontation would have resulted were it not for the farmers' wives—two law-abiding women who wouldn't think twice about having their husbands arrested. Spotting his wife watching from the doorway, Alphonse halted his attack on the flowers. Peter, too, stopped in his tracks as he recalled the horrified look on his wife's face as he pulled the illegal volume from the bookshelf. The two men smiled, tipped their hats, and belched with a force that sent the weather vane spinning atop Alphonse's barn.

Throughout town and countryside, gastric eruptions began occurring at an alarming rate—as many as two hundred per minute, reported one census taker. The subjects of Talkalot grew more miserable by the day. They walked around clutching their sides and chewing on mint leaves to help settle their churning stomachs. The demand for mint increased so dramatically, in fact, that the precious green stuff became scarce and was produced exclusively under close guard in the nearby District of Columbia.

As months turned to years, a noxious cloud began forming over the entire kingdom. The castle itself pumped tons of fumes into the air as the King and Queen faced the gastrointestinal challenges of raising a child. The heir to the throne was now seven years old and terribly fond of the phrase, "NO!" She applied it to each and every one of her parents' requests, from "Let your cousins out of the dungeon" to "Don't let your dragon breathe fire near your father's treaties."

Loving her above all else, however, the King and Queen bent the law a bit and allowed her to vent *her* anger in the privacy of her own room with the door locked and shades drawn. There the princess would snort and stomp around for hours until she was too worn out to do anything but think. Then she'd summon her parents to tell them exactly how she felt—which was difficult since the Royal Tutor had been ordered to coin new words for the lesson previously titled, "Our Amazing Emotions, from (A)nger to (Z)eal."

"I feel applesauce!" Winifryd declared. "I can't help it. You'd feel applesauce, too, if someone was always telling you 'Do this' and 'Don't do that' without ever telling you why."

The King and Queen listened—or tried to—over the noise coming from their stomachs, which, after seven years of forced agreeableness, sounded like a blacksmiths' convention.

"If your dragon keeps burning up my treaties," the King explained over the din, "the other monarchs must keep coming back to sign new ones. That eats up eight or nine months of their time, plus travel expenses. Some of them are getting pretty fed up."

"Well, why didn't you say so?" said the Princess. "I think I'll go ask cook to fix me a German sausage with lots of onions. Bye!"

Princess Winifryd had never had an upset stomach in her life.

The King and Queen soon noticed that they, too, always felt better after their little talks with Winifryd, though they had no idea why. But before they could figure it out, their stomachs would start acting up again. The King gagged to see the Queen floss her teeth at the Round Table, while the Queen hiccupped uncontrollably each time her husband left his best suit of armor out rusting in the rain.

"He has no idea how long it takes to re-oil that blasted suit week after week," she'd mumble to herself, as her stomach bloated to the size of a hippopotamus. Before long a plume of gas would rise from the castle, attracting the attention of farmers up to ten miles away.

The cloud over Talkalot eventually grew so thick that the people all stooped and slouched from the sheer weight of it pressing down upon their heads. It completely blocked out the sun and moon so that everyone lost track of the hours and seasons. Travel became difficult, at best, so few people ventured out of their houses without a very good reason.

No longer able to see their kingdom from their window, the King and Queen attempted to communicate with their subjects via carrier pigeon. What few fowl survived the noxious fumes returned to the castle with pleas for stricter air-quality control standards.

The palace quickly responded by summoning a team of Royal Scientists to conduct a comprehensive study of the problem. Six months later they presented their official findings:

> In short, there's simply not
> a more repugnant spot
> than Talkalot.
> Get out while you still can.

"Isn't there anything else we can do?" the King asked as the scientists were packing up to go.

The scientists all shook their heads and filed out of the castle. As the last one passed by the King, he leaned over and whispered, "There is one more thing you could try."

"Anything!" said the King.

"You could lift the ban on the Royal Physician," whispered the scientist. "If you can't eliminate the cloud, you might at least treat the effects."

The King watched the scientist disappear into the cloud with the others.

'Lift the ban?' he thought. No King before him had ever gone back on a decision, no matter how senseless or premature. Yet it was his own father who had said, as he was dressing for his eighth in a series of politically expedient marriages, "Desperate times call for desperate measures."

And so the King sent three Royal Knights to search for the Royal Physician and bring him back to the castle. Six months passed before they found him, at last, sitting cross-legged on a mountaintop, eating a bowl of tofu. Without further ado—actually, without any ado whatsoever—the knights stuffed him into a knapsack and returned to the castle, where they dumped him out rather unceremoniously on the throne-room floor before the entire court.

"Welcome home!" said the King.

"We've missed you," said the Queen.

The Royal Physician sat very still, not saying a word.

"Perhaps you'd like to freshen up after such a long trip," offered the Queen.

The Royal Physician remained silent.

"The man must be too angry to speak," the King whispered to the Queen.

"Surely we can put this banishing business behind us after all this time, can't we?" asked the Queen.

Again, the Royal Physician said nothing. Instead, he turned to them and smiled.

"What are you smiling at?" asked the King, feeling annoyed.

Silence, and more silence.

"I command you to tell me what you're smiling about!" the King repeated, his annoyance turning to anger.

A look of pure peace shone from the Royal Physician's face.

"That's it! Now you're really starting to tick me off!" shouted the King. The entire court gasped and then belched in unison.

The Royal Physician's peaceful presence seemed to have a disturbing effect upon the entire court, who felt that his silence, his stillness, and especially his ingratiating smile flew in the face of their obvious discomforts. The dukes and duchesses, counts and countesses, knights and maidens all began to twitch with anger. Then they started to shake. Even the court jester, unable to find any humor in the moment, shook so hard the bells jangled right off his cap.

Then it happened. Pandemonium.

All at once the room exploded in a rage. Men, women, and children all stomped around, shaking their fists. Some went whirling across the floor like dust devils kicked up by a spell of hot weather. Others leaped and turned somersaults in the air, while still others lay down and flailed their limbs against the carpet.

Everyone was screeching like a flock of jaybirds, calling out every angry word they could recall from the old days, before the law. The noise drifted out of the castle, through the town, and far into the fields.

Soon hundreds of town and country folk were making their way to the castle to find out what was going on. Before they knew it, farmers, millers, peddlers, and blacksmiths—along with butchers, bakers, and candlestick makers—were drawn into the frenzy like bees to a hive. The castle walls shook with the force of a thousand voices, sending chunks of stone crashing to the floor.

At the center of it all sat the Royal Physician, silent and radiant as the sun. The longer he sat there, the more his silence grew until it surrounded him completely.

The silence kept on growing, enveloping a scribe and his apprentice locked in a bitter wage dispute. It came over two sisters fighting over a suitor, circumscribed an entire family upset about the provisions of Uncle Yoseff's will, then descended on a group of scientists about to come to fisticuffs over which came first, the chicken or the egg. It even settled over the King and Queen, who were hurling insults at each other like never before.

The silence grew and grew, swallowing up all the name calling, nitpicking, ballyhoo, and bilge water until . . .

All was silent. No one spoke. No one moved. And no one knew for how long, for even time stopped. At last, there came one small voice. And the voice said, "What's for dinner?"

All heads turned toward Princess Winifryd, who had been standing in the doorway, unnoticed, for hours.

"I'm starved," she said.

"So am I," said the Royal Physician, getting to his feet. "Let's go fix ourselves a feast."

And with that, Princess Winifryd and the Royal Physician went off to the kitchen, leaving the others just standing around staring at each other.

Then little by little, something curious began to happen. A few people began to talk. A few others began to listen. Then a few more talked, and a few more listened. One by one the subjects of Talkalot found the courage to put words to their anger, warily at first, as though they were acknowledging a family secret in public for the first time.

Alphonse talked to Peter about his dogs. Genuinely sorry to hear how their barking had kept his neighbors awake every night, Peter promised to keep the animals quiet. For his part, Alphonse promised to replant his neighbor's garden forthwith.

Across the room, David was telling Mary he was sorry for taking over her corner, explaining that he was new in town and unfamiliar with the territory. Mary listened, apologized for her rude welcome, then suggested the two become partners in a mail-order fruit business.

"We'll call it 'Mary and David's,' " she said, and closed the deal with a handshake.

Everywhere the King and Queen looked, people were communicating with each other, some even without words. But even more incredible than what everyone was doing, was what they *weren't* doing.

They weren't belching. They weren't burping. They weren't hiccupping or urping.

The King and Queen simply didn't get it. Their own stomachs had begun to churn all over again at the very sight of each other, though they were now somewhat self-conscious about the fumes visibly rising from their lips. Taking a good hard swallow, they each held their breath.

A minute passed. Then two. Nearly thirty minutes went by before word began to spread throughout the room that something was terribly wrong.

One by one, the horrified subjects turned to find their King and Queen poised like a couple of frightened cobras ready to strike, their necks bulging to ten times their normal size from all the unspoken feelings lodged in their throats. Their condition well beyond the help of first aid, the King and Queen were immediately rushed to the Royal Infirmary.

Given the extreme nature of their condition, recovery was slow, but sure, nevertheless.

One morning Princess Winifryd, accompanied by the Royal Physician, came by to find her parents lost in conversation.

The King began,

> *My blood pressure rises*
> *When you floss your incisors*
> *Without looking to see*
> *If I've finished my tea.*
> *For my stomach is weak*
> *And my ire quick to peak.*
> *Still I regret all the same*
> *That I called you "Inane."*

To which the Queen replied,

> *I'm afraid, can't you see,*
> *That you won't notice me*
> *'Less I do something drastic*
> *Sure to stir something gastric.*
> *For my mother told me*
> *When I was but three*
> *"The way to a king's heart*
> *Is his stomach, you see."*

The King and Queen took each other's hands and gave a little squeeze as they vowed, in unison,

> *We hereby decree*
> *From this day to eternity*
> *We will share what we feel*
> *From anger to zeal*

Without shouting out names
Meant to pester and blame
Else we'll risk losing sight of
The power and might of
An unspoken intention
In the lower intestine.

"Excellent!" interrupted the Royal Physician. "Just a little more conversation, and you could be home by the end of the week."

The King and Queen looked hopeful.

"I lifted the edict, just like you asked," announced the Princess. "But could your other business wait until you get back? Arthur invited me to visit Camelot this afternoon."

Her parents joyfully sent her off with their blessings. Waving good-bye from the window, the King and Queen marveled at the clear blue sky.

Integration Reflections

Create a Space:

Grant yourself the gift of time by entering, leaving and re-entering the Integration Reflections as your spirit guides you. Weave the wonder of your experience at whatever pace you need to summon and integrate your inner wisdom. Each time you re-enter the Reflections, remind yourself to create a space.

Take a few deep breaths . . . allow yourself to feel supported with each new breath . . . feel the peace and safety of the space you are creating . . . most importantly, honor yourself just exactly as you are . . . simply notice, breathe, and become more aware of and connected with your body with each breath.

Play your personal "Create a Space" tape if you wish.

FEELINGS

The King and Queen thanked the Royal Physician for sharing his feelings, then promptly banished him for having raised his voice to them.

THERE AND THEN: "Going to Yellowstone is my first vacation, and I am very happy. I want to buy something to remind me of the trip forever. I go into the gift shop and see a ring with a black stone with a little silver bear on top. It is the kind of ring I can make fit my finger, and it is the neatest ring I ever remember seeing in my life. My mother looks at the tag that says how much it costs and tells me it will take all the vacation money I have. I am proud I have saved enough money to buy such a beautiful ring. I buy it, and all day long I stop and look at the ring while I play in the woods and feel butterflies in my stomach. I feel like the most special kid in the world. It is getting dark and time for bed. I decide to look at my ring one last time for the day. When I look at my finger, the ring is gone. I feel scared and sad and afraid to tell my mother because she didn't want me to spend all my money on just one thing. I cry all night and feel sick to my stomach. Early in the morning I go back to where I was playing and look for my ring. I can't find it any place. Finally I tell my mother about the ring. I can't believe I can feel so many feelings in my body all in one day. It makes me very tired, and I cry until I fall asleep on her lap."

HERE AND NOW: "Over the years the labels and places in my body where I am aware of my feelings have changed, even if the feeling is the same. Feeling scared was in my belly as a child. As I grew, I labeled feeling scared as 'being afraid.' Being afraid was in my chest. Now I label being afraid as 'fear,' and fear is in my throat. I continue to explore different labels for my feelings. I am learning to trust the wisdom of my body to help me clarify my feelings."

Insight:

▶ In your journal, make a list of as many feeling words as you can think of. Use letters of the alphabet to prompt feeling words. Write the first thing that comes into your mind for each letter: A=anger, B=bubbly, C=cunning, D=daring, E=emotional, F=fear . . . Z=zeal.

▶ Study your list and select five or more feeling words that have the most power for you. Take your time.

▶ Write each selected feeling word on separate pieces of paper or note cards. You may choose to write each word in a color that reminds you of that feeling.
For example: On one note card I write the word "anger" in red letters. On another card I write the word "peace" in green. Another card has the word "hope" in yellow.

Integration:

▶ Gather your "feeling cards" and take them on a walk with you in nature and/or around your house. Choose an item or symbol for each feeling word.
For example: a cotton ball for "peace," a shell for "joy," a thorn from a bush for "anger," a leaf for "joy," a stuffed animal for "happy."

▶ Draw or color a large outline or stick figure of your body big enough to provide space for arranging the "feeling symbols" you have gathered.

▶ As you hold each "feeling symbol," allow your mind to scan your body, making no judgment of right or wrong, good or bad. Invite the feeling the object symbolizes to enter your body/mind.

▶ Make a "Body Map of Feelings" by placing each "feeling symbol" and "feeling card" on the drawing of your body in the area that seems to match your experience.
For example: As I study the drawing of my body, I place a black rock on my throat with the card "fear." I place a leaf on my chest with the card "joy." I place a thorny branch and its card on my abdomen for "anger."

▶ Share your "Body Map of Feelings" with another person, if it feels right. Journal about the experience of creating your "Body Map."

STUFFING

The word soon spread across the land that anger was no longer permissible among the subjects . . . Throughout town and countryside, gastric eruptions began occurring at an alarming rate . . . The subjects of Talkalot grew more miserable by the day. They walked around clutching their sides and chewing on mint leaves to help settle their churning stomachs.

THERE AND THEN: "I see my neighbor throw rocks at my dog, Brownie. I have a feeling inside that is different. I want to throw a rock at my neighbor. I want him to stop being bad to my dog. My mother says I can't throw a rock at my neighbor or even tell him to not throw one at Brownie. She says Brownie shouldn't go into his yard. I mix something with my chemistry set that smells really bad and leave it in his mail box. I don't say 'hello' or smile at him anymore. I wonder why I can't just tell him not to throw rocks at my dog."

HERE AND NOW: "I ask a friend what I look like and what I do when I'm angry and stuffing my feelings. She tells me my face turns red and gets tight; I walk away and get quiet; I don't smile; I act cold; occasionally I slam a door and swear more. On the inside I feel frightened. The feeling starts in my stomach and radiates to my arms and legs. I feel like I want to run, but I'm stuck. Sometimes I cry."

Insight:

▶ Study your "Body Map," noticing all the symbols.

▶ Select one of the symbols that represents a "stuffed feeling," one you are most likely not to express when you feel it. Take your time.

▶ Find a comfortable place and hold your feeling symbol in your hand. Allow your mind to return to child-time. . . .

▶ When you feel ready, journal about the history of that "stuffed feeling" in your life. When or how did you feel the "stuffed feeling"? How did you learn to stuff the feeling? What do you do with the stuffed feeling today? What happens to your body/mind when you do not allow yourself to express the stuffed feeling?

Integration:

▶ Position your symbol for the stuffed feeling in a place where you can see it. Read your history of this stuffed feeling out loud from your journal, allowing the symbol to hear about its history in your life.

▶ Recall a recent time when you were unable to express your stuffed feeling. . . . Allow the details of that experience to enter your body/mind.

▶ When you are ready, allow your body to move with the feeling, using postures, gestures and sounds of the stuffed feeling.

▶ When your movement is complete, journal about what happens in your body/mind when you experience a stuffed feeling.

EXPRESSING

We hereby decree
From this day to eternity
We will share what we feel
From anger to zeal
Without shouting out names
Meant to pester and blame
Else we'll risk losing sight of
The power and might of
An unspoken intention
In the lower intestine.

THERE AND THEN: "I find a dollar underneath my mother's bed and hide it in my room. I have never had that much money before. Later I take it to the store and pick out lots of things my mother never lets me eat. I give the dollar to Mr. Evans, the man who owns the store, and he asks me where I got all that money. I tell him a lie about my grandfather giving it to me. Mr. Evans looks at my face and says my face looks like I am not telling the truth. I cry and tell him the truth. He tells me to go home and talk to my mother. He gives me a piece of candy for telling the truth. I go home and tell my mother about the dollar, and she gives me a hug for telling her the truth. I decide I like telling truth."

HERE AND NOW: "Years later my mother told me Mr. Evans called her about the money, and she had other than a hug in mind if I hadn't told her about it. When I was a child, expressing feelings was an easy thing to do. As Mr. Evans and many others since have told me, my face expresses my feelings."

Insight:

▶ Look at your "Body Map." Along with the symbol you selected for a stuffed feeling, select another symbol to join it that represents an "easy feeling," one you most easily express.

▶ Breathe in the essence of your "easy feeling." When you are ready, journal about the history of that feeling in your life. When or how did you feel the easy feeling? How did you learn to express the feeling? What do you do with the easy feeling today? What happens to your body/mind when you allow yourself to express the easy feeling?

▶ Compare the history of your "stuffed feeling" with the history of the "easy feeling" and journal about similarities and differences in their histories.

Integration:

▶ Hold your symbol of an "easy feeling" and recall a recent time when you were in a situation expressing this feeling. . . .

▶ Allow your body to move with the feeling, using postures and gestures. Add sounds or words to your movement.

▶ When your movement is complete, re-read the history of the feeling you most likely stuff, and breathe in the energy of that history.

▶ Invite your body to move with the combination of energy from the history of the stuffed feeling and energy of the easily expressed feeling.

▶ Journal about what occurred when you combined patterns of expression of the two feelings.

COMMUNICATING

Then little by little, something curious began to happen. A few people began to talk. A few others began to listen. Then a few more talked, and a few more listened . . . Everywhere the King and Queen looked, people were communicating with each other, some even without words.

THERE AND THEN: "My mother's face doesn't look like my mother. Her eyes are too little, and her mouth turns down. She walks away from me and shuts the door with a loud sound. I feel scared, like I have done something really bad that made my mother go away. Later my mother tells me she was angry because I was in her room. I still feel scared and tell her I don't like her face when it looks like that. I want her to use more words when I don't do what she likes."

HERE AND NOW: "When I do something that displeases my friends and family, I prefer direct communication about what is happening. When I don't get the communication I need about a situation, I still start out feeling scared. But now I keep asking questions until I feel better. The discomfort about the situation gives me the energy to bring it to a resolution."

Insight:

▶ Study your "Body Map," again noticing all the powerful feelings it contains.

▶ Write a journal entry for each of the feelings you identified in your "Body Map," describing the role each plays in blocking and helping you communicate with others.
For example: Anger blocks me when I walk away and helps me by the energy it gives me to speak my mind. Joy blocks me from noticing others' reactions and helps me express positive thoughts and feelings.

▶ Study your journal entries from this chapter and select one feeling that routinely and most powerfully blocks your ability to communicate.

▶ Recall a recent "blocked communication" situation when that feeling was present. Journal about the details of the experience. . . . Who was there? What words were spoken or not spoken? What kind of nonverbal "body language" was present? What was happening in your body?

Integration:

▶ Re-read your journal entry about a recent "blocked communication." Allow the wholeness and energy of that experience to enter your body/mind.

▶ Select a color that best expresses the power of the situation and begin to color the experience. Keep coloring until the energy from the experience fades. Do not try to "do" anything with the energy, just keep coloring, allowing it to shift and change. You can close your eyes if you wish. As you notice a shift, select another color that matches the change.

▶ Study your coloring, noticing the shifts and changes the colors represent. Begin to form in your mind words you would use to describe the shifts and changes.

▶ Invite yourself to use the words of your coloring to write a personal fable about feelings, stuffing, expressing, and communicating. You may find it helpful to arrange the beginning and middle of your fable, then keep writing until a resolution to unblocking communication appears. As with the coloring, keep writing until you experience an "ending," a resolution to the blocked communication. Invite yourself to set aside your writing and/or coloring until the resolution appears. Give your fable a title.

▶ Offer yourself time for writing and/or coloring an "ending" whenever a "blocked communication" may occur.

VI
A Crystal Flute

𝕿his is the story of Marcelle, the one-woman band of Pythagoras County.

Our tale begins, not at the beginning, but in the middle, on the morning Marcelle awoke in a field of wild daisies to discover that her life had been stolen right out from under her nose. Until then, Marcelle's life had consisted of a trombone, harmonica, snare drum, three pairs of drumsticks, one set of castanets, and a knapsack stuffed with songbooks. While that may not sound like much of a life, consider the questions that ran through Marcelle's mind: What future exists for a one-woman band without any instruments? What chance for recognition? What hope for harmony?

More than anything in the world, Marcelle wanted to be one-half of a duo, an equal part in a perfect two-part harmony. To that end, Marcelle commanded an impressive solo repertoire designed to please most of the people most of the time, thus maximizing her chances of attracting a lifelong musical companion.

As time went by, she learned to accommodate more and more audience requests until she could play everything from reggae to ragtime. She even knew the music to forty-seven college fight songs in case anyone should ask. Yet even as her repertoire, general popularity, and income steadily grew, so did the empty feeling in her heart.

Fate seemingly turned a deaf ear to Marcelle's music and her desires, leaving her alone and searching for companionship.

"I fear I'll remain alone and searching for the rest of my life," she was fond of saying, though the only grain of truth lay in the words "I fear."

So at the sight of crushed daisies where her instruments had rested the night before, Marcelle's fear became almost too much to bear. The only possessions the thieves had left behind were the only ones she no longer had use for: a sheet music holder (her own invention) that looked like a crown with antennae, and a crystal flute she hadn't played since childhood.

Marcelle picked up her crown and plunked it on her head, the music to "It's My Party (I'll Cry If I Want To)" still clipped to one of the antennae. 'What now, old girl?' she asked herself.

That's a very good question, love. Let me think about that a minute, Herself answered.

'Don't take too long,' said Marcelle.

The way I see it, Herself said, *we can either head on up the road, or go back the way we came.*

'What possible good could come from going on?' asked Marcelle, looking beyond the daisies to a dusty, deserted road.

Back the way we came then, Herself answered, trying to be agreeable.

'Back the way we came?' Marcelle whispered, tears welling in her eyes. 'It's too late. I don't remember how we got here. I don't know the way back.'

Before Herself had a chance to respond, a curious thing happened. A tornado that had just swept through Kansas—carrying off houses, trees, and, according to eyewitnesses, even a witch on a bicycle —touched down in Marcelle's field. Before she knew what was happening, a shutter that had been torn off its hinges blew past and hit her in the head.

What was even more curious, when she came to, she was a child again back in Pythagoras County, back with her parents, her great uncle, two brothers, and a maiden aunt—back where it all began. Marcelle marched back into the past without missing a beat, completely unaware that she had ever left.

In Marcelle's past, every day was devoted to school. Every evening, Marcelle and the other family members all assembled in the parlor for a family musicale. Solos were discouraged. Rather, the purpose of these ensembles was to teach the children the three "ize": Harmonize, Synchronize, or else Apologize.

Early settlers had named Pythagoras County after one of the first mathematicians ever to hear the "music of the spheres," an ethereal symphony created by the natural movement of heavenly bodies. It was the founders' intent to outlaw committees altogether and to start a community in harmony with the *natural* order of the universe. Alas, somehow or other, later generations missed the point.

And so, with Marcelle on washboard, her father on fiddle, her mother on piano, and the others on a surprisingly melodious array of cookware, Marcelle learned the finer points of keeping in step.

Then one day something magical happened. While walking in the woods near her family's cottage, Marcelle happened upon a lovely, sun-washed glade. There she found a crystal flute lying half-hidden in a patch of daisies. Looking around to be sure no one was watching, she picked up the flute, put it to her lips, and blew.

There came a hollow rush of air. She tried again. A faint squeak. She tried once more, and a note as clear and true as a diamond graced the morning. Startled, Marcelle dropped the flute and ran for fear the rightful owner would catch her playing it.

She returned to the glade every day for the next week. And every day the flute was right where she had left it. At last she carried the crystal flute into town to see if she could find its rightful owner. Everyone in town took a turn trying to play it, including a squire named Arthur and three wicked stepsisters with big feet. Yet no matter how others tried, the crystal flute would play for no one but Marcelle.

Finally satisfied that no one was ever coming to claim the flute, Marcelle kept it for her own, returning to the glade every day to play. Unearthly melodies began to flow from her as naturally as breathing, as though she herself were but an instrument of some invisible, otherworldly musician. Happening upon an Easter lily in the middle of December could not have surprised her more than the birth of each new melody. Many times she would return home eager to share some new creation with her family.

"I wrote a new melody today," she would announce. "Can I play it for you?"

"Not now, honey," said her father. "I'm busy making a living."

"Maybe later, darling," said her mother. "I'm busy trying to take care of everyone's needs all at once."

"I'm busy trying to find a project to make me feel useful," said her great uncle.

"I'm getting gussied up to go look for a husband," said her aunt Hermione. "I have to . . . OUCH! . . . pluck my . . . OUCH! . . . eyebrows. Women must always be . . . OUCH! . . . prepared to sacrifice for . . . OUCH! . . . beauty. Never forget that, my dear. OUCH!"

Her brothers said simply, "Wait your turn, squirt. We were here first."

Marcelle accepted her family's refusals with quiet disappointment, working even harder each evening to harmonize with them. She began to notice that everyone seemed most pleased with her (and themselves) when keeping time to the same old tunes. As the years went by, Marcelle played her flute in the glade less and less until she quit playing altogether. She grew lonely and sad.

Then one day Lorenzo, a one-man band, came through Pythagoras County. Marcelle was resting on a park bench as a crowd of people marched past, stepping to the steady "BOOM, BOOM, BOOM" of a base drum with "Loveable Lorenzo" painted on the side. Lorenzo led the crowd to the town square where he entertained everyone for hours with a string of familiar tunes.

Everyone loved Lorenzo. At least, that's the way it appeared to Marcelle. Children from toddlers to teenagers giggled and wiggled to the music, while the grown-ups sang along. Single women looked upon him longingly, each one hoping to catch his eye, to be the one to end his wanderings. Especially Aunt Hermoine.

"Isn't he a dream?" she cooed as Lorenzo answered a request to play Rossini's "Barber of Seville" on the accordion. "Simply a dream."

'Loveable Lorenzo must never feel sad or lonely,' thought Marcelle, looking around at all the faces beaming in approval. 'I want to be just like him,' she told herself. 'I want to play whatever people want to hear so that they will always listen. I want adoring boys to fight for the chance to become my accompanist. I can endure a little time alone on the road if a companion awaits at the end. I want to become a one-woman band.'

It's too bad Marcelle wasn't around a few hours later as Lorenzo packed up his things and trudged on toward the next town. Had she seen his face—skin pale and drawn, eyes dull and hollow—Marcelle might have given her decision a bit more thought. Unfortunately, the course in "The Importance of Seeing the Big Picture" had long ago been dropped from the high school curriculum in favor of "How to Avoid Being Single in Society."

And so, with scarcely a lemming's insight into what she was in for, Marcelle embarked on her new career. On the morning of her eighteenth birthday, she took her piggy bank to the music store and bought the best instruments she could afford. Next she outfitted them with straps and buckles, then practiced toting them over various types of terrain until her legs, back, and shoulders were as solid as month-old muffins. After conducting a thorough demographic study of song preferences, Marcelle kissed her family good-bye and set off for a town called Hamelin where rumor had it that another self-employed musician had achieved instant fame.

While the citizens of Hamelin proved to be unwelcoming (though well-armed with an impressive arsenal of rotten fruit), Marcelle remained undaunted, hoping against hope that her happiness lay in the next town, the next audience, the next pair of eyes she gazed into. Remembering what her Aunt Hermoine had said about the importance of beauty, Marcelle frequently took her trombone from the case, considered her reflection in the bell, then plucked her eyebrows until they were two perfect, throbbing arches.

'You just never know when a good partner may happen along,' she reasoned.

Along one particularly memorable—and muddy—stretch of road, she came upon a series of one-man bands who at first seemed to be traveling in her direction. The first was Downbeat Donahue, a tall, lanky musician given to playing slow, plodding dirges with titles like "Requiem for the Passions of Youth," "Saturnine, Opus 104," and "Ain't No Color in My Kaleidoscope."

At first Marcelle was grateful for Donahue's company. Like generations of Pythagorites before her, Marcelle had been taught that "Something is always preferable to nothing" (another time-altered creed bearing little resemblance to the original, which was, "Give nothing, receive nothing"). So while Marcelle didn't especially care for Donahue's musical leanings, she assumed even *his* company was preferable to none at all. Before she knew it, she found herself playing along, day after day, note after note after slow, plodding, depressing note. In time, her legs and her heart grew so heavy, she began to sink up to her knees in the muddy road.

Longing for higher ground and happier tunes, Marcelle at last asked Donahue to go on without her.

"I expected as much," he said, trudging away through the mud.

'If I ever meet up with Donahue again, it will be too soon,' thought Marcelle, struggling to pull herself out of the mire.

"Allow me," said a voice. Marcelle looked up at the face of Responsible Rooney, another one-man band who offered to carry Marcelle's instruments until she got back on her feet. Marcelle welcomed his assistance—that is, until she'd walked a full twenty miles listening to him complain about the added burden. When she offered to take back her share of the load, he protested even more.

"The responsibility of shouldering heavy burdens is mine and mine alone," sighed Rooney, his face lined with pain and his back shaped like a question mark.

"Why?" asked Marcelle.

"Why?" he echoed. "Well, uh, um, I don't exactly know *why*. I just *know*, that's all. What have you got in these cases? Bricks?"

Being young and somewhat naïve, Marcelle was quick to take Rooney's bravado as a sign of superior strength and capability. As the miles went on, she depended on him more and more. She began to think she simply couldn't manage without his help.

If only he didn't complain so much!

"Oh, my aching feet . . . Oh, my aching knees . . . Oh, my aching hips," he moaned, stooping a bit more with each step.

Marcelle felt an uncomfortable sensation in the pit of her stomach. It felt like guilt.

"Oh, my aching back . . . Oh, my aching shoulders . . . Oh, my aching neck . . . Oh, my . . ."

"I think we both could use a little fun," Marcelle interrupted. "Let's rest awhile and play a duet on our harmonicas."

"Some other time, perhaps," said Rooney. "My responsibilities come first."

Indeed, each passing mile brought even more responsibility as Rooney took on the burdens of every farmer, peddler, and carrier pigeon he met. Before long his shoulders were piled high with instruments, hay seed, live turkeys, cases of Dr. Pinkham's Improved Liver Pills, and top-secret documents bound for heads of state. The effort to balance it all drained the energy and cheer from his body, leaving little to play duets with Marcelle.

At every crossroads Marcelle considered parting ways, but somehow even Rooney seemed preferable to going it alone. That is, until the moment Rooney stumbled and found himself buried under several hundred pounds of responsibility. Now others might respond to such a calamity by taking some long overdue time to rest and reflect, but not Rooney. Barely fifteen minutes later, a fish monger came along, and Rooney insisted on carrying the man's stainless steel icebox containing three fifty-pound sturgeon.

The sight of Rooney struggling to his feet filled Marcelle with sadness and pity. It occurred to her that in all the miles they had walked together, Rooney had played no tunes, sung no songs, nor heard a single note of hers. He scarcely even noticed when Marcelle lifted her songbooks and instruments from his shoulders and swung them back onto her own.

And so, at the next fork in the road, Marcelle and Rooney simply drifted apart.

"If I ever meet up with Donahue or Rooney again, it will be too soon," sighed Marcelle. "I need a musician with infinite range. High notes, low notes, the whole shebang."

Marcelle didn't know it, but she was about to learn one of the great lessons of the road: Be very careful what you ask for.

Hearing an unusual noise, Marcelle turned to see what looked like a patch of fog on legs coming up the road.

"Who are you?" she asked as the fog reached her.

"I'm thirsty," said the fog. "Excuse me a moment while I take a drink."

A hand holding a well-worn wineskin appeared from out of the fog, then disappeared where Marcelle assumed the fog's mouth to be.

"Aghhhhhhhh," groaned the fog. "Much better. In fact, I feel a song coming on. Shall I play for you?"

Before Marcelle could even answer, notes poured from inside the mist like bubbles from a bubble machine. High notes, low notes, short notes, and long notes emerged as a pleasant, if somewhat rambling, melody that set Marcelle's feet to tapping. As the musician's playing continued, however, it became increasingly loud and fractured, frequently broken by long drinks from the wineskin.

The "song" went on, circling overhead like a flock of crows. Some of the notes began to cry. Others laughed and called Marcelle unkind names, while still others turned angry and mean. They came at her like hailstones until she was forced to run for cover.

"Leave me alone," she cried. "Please leave me alone!"

Shielding her head as best she could, Marcelle ran toward a distant stand of trees. She looked back only once, just long enough to see the fog lift for an instant and to look into the sad, lonely eyes of . . . Loveable Lorenzo!

"Come back," he called out to her. "I didn't mean to hurt you. I never mean to hurt anyone. It's just that I'm so unhappy, so lonely, and so very, very lost."

Marcelle ran and ran until she could run no farther. She fell exhausted into a field of flowers still crying, "Leave me alone, leave me alone, leave me alone."

All was quiet. Marcelle uncovered her face and looked around. No notes. No Lorenzo. No one. For the first time in a great while, she was alone in the silence.

Taking a long, deep breath, Marcelle closed her eyes and thought about Lorenzo. What had happened to him? Whatever could have turned his music so sour? How could he, given so much talent and attention, feel as lost and lonely as she? Pondering these questions, yet finding no answers, Marcelle fell fast asleep.

Then came the thieves, followed by the tornado, and once again, Marcelle awoke in the field of daisies—this time with a nasty bump on her head.

'Perfect,' she said to herself. 'What's next? Earthquake? Famine? Plague?'

You're doing it again, Herself answered.

'What? Tell me what. Exactly what is it I'm doing?' she said, clearly agitated with herself.

Feeling sorry for me.

'I can't help it,' said Marcelle. 'I'm so bewildered, I can't see the daisies for the crabgrass anymore.'

If I might make a suggestion, I suggest we be still awhile. Just watch and listen for signs.

'Signs?' Marcelle asked herself. 'Road signs? Picket signs? Signs of the zodiac?'

I'm not sure, but I just bet we'll know it when we see it.

'Why should I listen to you?' asked Marcelle. 'Since when have you been so wise?'

Since the day you were born.

Marcelle smiled. 'I don't suppose I have anything to lose by trying,' she said. So taking a deep breath, she closed her eyes and waited.

And waited, and waited.

Suddenly something moved in the grass. Marcelle opened her eyes to see where the rustling sound was coming from.

"Lorenzo? Is that you?"

The rustling sound came again.

"Go away! Leave me alone!" she called out.

Again came the sound of something stirring in the grass, this time at Marcelle's feet. She looked down, and WHOOSH! the crystal flute jumped right into her hands. Marcelle's eyes opened wide, and her hands began to tremble.

'Wwwwwhat now, old girl?' she asked herself.

Don't be afraid.

'Who did this? Who put this flute in my hands?'

You did, years ago when you found it in the glade. Don't you remember?

'Well, it's no good to me now. Not now, when my life is in shambles.'

What of then? What good did it hold for you then?

Marcelle tried to recall. Minutes passed, then hours. She turned the flute over and over in her hands, watching how the light reflected off the delicate crystal. The longer she held it, the more miraculous it seemed. Silent and neglected, it had somehow survived the miles, the treacherous roads, the years of accompanying all her fears, doubts, and disappointments from one county to the next.

At last, at sunset, Marcelle raised the flute to her lips. There came a hollow rush of air. She tried again. A faint squeak. She tried once more, and a note as clear and true as a diamond graced the evening.

A feeling of joy and wonderment came over her that was at once familiar and new, for in its sound lived her mother and her father, her great uncle, her aunt, and her brothers.

In its sound lived the seasons and citizens of Pythagoras County, as well as her time with Donahue, Rooney, and Lorenzo.

In its sound lived joy and sorrow, courage and fear, wonderment and pain. The more Marcelle played, the wiser she became until, at last, she could clearly see the road behind and the promise of the road ahead.

Yet she chose neither.

For now it was enough—no, it was everything—to be alone in a meadow, playing to the music of the spheres.

Integration Reflections

Create a Space:

Grant yourself the gift of time by entering, leaving and re-entering the Integration Reflections as your spirit guides you. Weave the wonder of your experience at whatever pace you need to summon and integrate your inner wisdom. Each time you re-enter the Reflections, remind yourself to create a space.

> Invite your mind to become quiet, to relax along with the rest of you . . . let your mind know you will take care of any concerns it has later . . . let any external sounds deepen your state of relaxation . . . if you like, invite your spirit as a guide for exactly what you need.

You may wish to play your "Create a Space" tape to further enjoy your mind/body relaxation.

DISCOVERY

There she found a crystal flute lying half-hidden in a patch of daisies . . . She picked up the flute, put it to her lips, and blew . . . She tried once more, and a note as clear and true as a diamond graced the morning.

THERE AND THEN: "I discover a jungle across the fields from my house. I name it the 'Bird Jungle.' There are a lot of birds, frogs, and snakes. All these things I love to watch and sometimes catch for a closer look. Sometimes I take things home to show my mother. This time, when I give her my dad's handkerchief full of baby water snakes, she falls on the floor. My dad says she fainted. I feel bad and alone, so I go back to the 'jungle' and watch things there. I hear the wind in the trees, and I feel better."

HERE AND NOW: "I sit under grandfather tree, playing my flute and hearing the wind in the massive old branches. I seek out this special place to feel grounded, more like 'me.' I have always discovered places in nature where I feel safe and renewed."

Insight:

▶ Allow yourself to return to child-time. . . . Recall discovering a place, item, or activity that was a special part of your childhood.

▶ In your journal, describe its "specialness." How did you discover it? How did it comfort you, allow you to feel joy, feel special? With whom did you share it?

Integration:

▶ Give yourself permission to re-create your childhood "discovery" experience now. Allow yourself to fill with the wonderment.

▶ Design a way to keep the feeling with you for the rest of these reflections.
For example: Turn your discovery into a color, put it on a list, create a special place inside you to "carry" it, select an item of jewelry or clothing as a symbol and wear it.

MESSAGES

Solos were discouraged. Rather, the purpose of these ensembles was to teach the children the three "ize": Harmonize, Synchronize, or else Apologize.

THERE AND THEN: "My mother says: 'You are the girl in the family so you can't do what your brothers do. If you always beat them at tennis, they won't like you. Your father is too busy this year to take you hunting; maybe next year when you are older. People in this family go to church on Sundays.' "

HERE AND NOW: "I struggle with who I am, both connected to and separate from the messages I received growing up. When I challenge an old family message, I feel a lot like when I was a child trying to 'fit' in my family. I feel confused for a time while my adult-self decides whether the message is one I want to repeat."

Insight:

▶ Allow yourself to return to child-time. . . . Picture yourself interacting with your family, possibly at the dinner table or playing a game.

▶ Write in your journal the most frequent messages you received. What messages did you hear when you were excited to show or tell something? What were the messages about family/gender roles (father, mother, grandfather, grandmother, older or younger siblings; how boys or girls are expected to be)? What were the messages about how to attract a mate/life partner?

- Focus on one message you received that has the most power for you as you write about it, perhaps a message that challenges you or one that enhances your life.

- As you journal details of the message, stay in touch with feelings and thoughts you had as a child when you received the message and those you have now as an adult.

Integration:

- On one side of a piece paper, write the "child" message. On the other side, write an "adult" message that challenges, or is opposite to, the child message.
  For example: Side one reads, "Girls can't do what boys do." Side two reads, "Girls and boys are free to choose what they want to do."

- Study the message on one side of the paper and allow it to be fully present with you. Breathe in the thoughts, feelings, and senses of the message. Invite your body to move into a shape that fits what you are experiencing. Allow yourself to make a sound that fits.

- While maintaining the internal sense of the message, write or color, what you are experiencing. Move into and out of the body shape or make the sound several times while writing about/coloring the experience.

- Now focus on the message on the opposite side of the paper and repeat the exercise.

- Journal/color about the experience. What changes? What remains the same?

DIRECTION

More than anything in the world, Marcelle wanted to be one-half of a duo, an equal part in a perfect two-part harmony . . . And so, with scarcely a lemming's insight into what she was in for, Marcelle embarked on her new career.

THERE AND THEN: "My mother asks me, 'What do you want to be when you grow up?' At five, I say, 'A cowboy.' At six, I say, 'An Indian.' At eight, I answer, 'A wife and mother of five.' At ten, I am proud to announce, 'A tin smith, like my dad and brothers.' At twelve, 'A teacher.' At fifteen, 'A teacher.' At eighteen, 'A wife, a mother, and a teacher.' "

HERE AND NOW: "At twenty-one, 'I think I'll join the Navy.' At twenty-five, 'I've decided to go back to school.' At thirty, 'Okay, I'll take the job as a drug and alcohol counselor until I solve the alcohol problem in Idaho, then I'll go back to teaching.' At forty, 'I'm unemployed and insecure; I think I'll get a Ph.D.' At forty-five, 'I've been in therapy long enough; I think I'll be a therapist.' At fifty, I say 'A therapist, maybe I'll write a book, maybe retire early, be a teacher, maybe . . .' "

Insight:

▸ Locate the "Dream and Wish Map" you created after the Jarviss Fidget story. Study the map. Focus on experiences that helped you decide on your life direction.

▸ Journal about the influences and experiences. Notice if there are any patterns or recurring themes. Note how you are guided now in your life direction. How does what you do in your life fit with how you *are* as a person?

Integration:

▸ Find an old pair of shoes that you do not wear anymore. Study the shoes and picture in your mind how you have "traveled" in them. Where have you walked in them? Who have you walked with? What pain and/or pleasure have you experienced while wearing them?

▸ Locate some appropriate shoe-decorating materials (glue, scissors, an old edition of a favorite magazine, tin foil, cotton balls, magic markers, etc.) Decorate one shoe to represent the journey of the "road behind." Decorate the other shoe to represent the "road ahead."

▸ Put on a pair of socks that reminds you of today. Choose a color to match the "color" of your imagination. Slip your feet into your "road behind" and "road ahead" shoes. Take a few minutes to relax and breathe in the experiences of your life.

▸ Allow your shoes to take you on a walk around the room. You may wish to use some of the Integration Reflections you have already experienced in this book to help guide your movement.
For example: Notice how your shoes call you to move, forward or backward, with the voice of "patience" (page 26), the color of "lost" (page 28), the feeling of "different" (page 30), the celebration of "potential" (page 32), the feeling of "renewal" (page 48), the "gifts of aging" (page 60), the thank-you to "joy" (page 76), the gift of "feelings" (page 88). Move as long as it feels right to continue.

▸ What do your shoes tell you? Journal/color the messages and share them with a fellow "traveler."

REDISCOVERY

"Who did this? Who put this flute in my hands?" . . . The longer she held it, the more miraculous it seemed. Silent and neglected, it had somehow survived . . . At last, at sunset, Marcelle raised the flute to her lips . . . A feeling of joy and wonderment came over her that was at once familiar and new . . . In its sound lived joy and sorrow, courage and fear . . . The more Marcelle played, the wiser she became.

A COMING TOGETHER OF "THERE AND THEN" WITH "HERE AND NOW": "When I was young, it seemed like everything worthwhile was in the 'someday.' Now I celebrate 'someday' everyday. I breathe in the experiences of my life and honor the color, shape, and movement that is present. I know well the 'road behind' and the promise of the 'road ahead.' It is in 'the now' that I rediscover me."

Insight:

▶ Take your time and recall special childhood feelings of discovery that you journaled about at the beginning of these chapter reflections (page 106). . . .

▶ Journal about how, when, or if you rediscovered the feeling while experiencing these reflections.

▶ Review your "Dream and Wish Map" and explore in your journal the wisdom that hindsight has granted you. What experiences would you repeat? What experiences would you leave out? Are there any "hindsight gifts" you need to rediscover?

Integration:

▶ Put on the color of your imagination, your "today" socks, and your "road behind" and "road ahead" pair of shoes. Craft a "Rediscovery" fable that captures the essence of your life. You may wish to use parts of the fables you have already written to assist you.

▶ Read your new fable out loud to yourself. Give it a title. Experience how it reflects the essence of your life.

▶ Celebrate by sharing your fable with friends and family.

▶ You may wish to invite others to a presentation, make an audio or video tape, or create a book with an illustrated cover for your fable.

Keep opening your heart
to your own wisdom.
It is always there for the knowing,
in the weaving.

Appendix

Making a "Create a Space" Tape

If you want to make your own tape for the "Create a Space" portions of the Integration Reflections, use the following script or any portion of it.* Record it in your own voice or ask a friend to speak on the recording.

As you record, let your voice resonate from its center in the lower belly. Pause at the ellipses.

————

Begin by slowing everything down . . .

Take a few deep breaths,
inhaling through your nose,
feeling the breath come from deep in your lower belly,
exhaling out through your mouth,
allowing any sighs and sounds . . .
Breathe in relaxing, calming energy,
exhaling out whatever you don't need . . .

Simply watch your breath, becoming more and more mindful . . .

Relaxing a little more with each breath,
let yourself go deeper and deeper inside,
feeling supported,
making this space a safe and peaceful place . . .

* Script courtesy of Pam DeLeo, licensed massage therapist in Coeur d'Alene, Idaho. Pam combines bodywork with guided visualization, breathwork, and emotional processing tools to provide integrative sessions. The script is also available on audio tape. See page 125 for information.

Let any external sounds deepen your state of relaxation,
allowing your breath to do the work,
supporting and containing the process for you . . .
Continue to let your breath become a little deeper, a little slower . . .
Allow your body to be breathed in its own rhythm . . .

Give yourself permission to fully experience
what you may need today . . .
Allow everything unimportant to drift away,
inviting your mind to rest as well . . .

With the next few breaths,
scan slowly up through your body,
noticing how each area feels . . .

Begin with your feet as you inhale;
feel and see your breath move into your feet.
Notice how they are, or suggest they relax as you breathe out . . .
Move up into your calves and knees,
into your thighs and pelvic area,
into your back,
into your torso and shoulders,
into your arms and hands,
into your neck and head and face and scalp . . .
Take a few more deep breaths;
notice if your body feels differently
and allow yourself to relax even more deeply . . .

When you are ready, breathe into your heart . . .
Give yourself permission to notice all the feelings
that are present and/or just below the surface . . .
You may want to welcome your unconscious,
allowing more into consciousness . . .

Continue to follow your breathing;
breathe into the feelings with acceptance . . .

Take a few deep breaths for clearing;
notice any mental concerns you may still have . . .

Breathe into the spirit within;
notice that part of you . . .
You might want to invite your Inner Wisdom
to guide what you need . . .

Continue to follow your breath
until you complete this journey . . .

Other possibilities:

1. *Breathe in a one-word quality that describes*
   what you want to feel,
     such as balance, peace, joy, or relaxation.
   Breathe out a one-word quality that describes
   what you want to release,
     such as fear or judgment.

2. A short version:

   Take a few deep breaths . . .
   Scan your body and pick an area you would like to work with . . .
   Focus on that area . . .
   Notice the different sensations, physical and non-physical . . .
   Ask your body if these sensations have any messages for you . . .
   Thank your body for its wisdom
   and continue to be aware of your breath . . .

Journaling

Journaling is simply writing and/or coloring your feelings and thoughts in a notebook or journal. Journaling is a tool to experience a dialogue with yourself that can reveal feelings lying beneath surface thought. Set your critical mind aside; do not concern yourself with spelling, punctuation, grammar, complete sentences, neatness or "style." Focus on the concept, reflection, thought, feeling, or movement you wish to explore and let whatever comes from inside guide your journaling. The use of color can expand the "vocabulary" of journal writing. Grant yourself permission to add color to your writing to capture more fully what is occurring for you.

We encourage you to expand your experience by sharing your journaling at different stages of the book, but remember you are writing only for you. The choice to share, or not share, journal entries is entirely yours. Most of all, enjoy the surprises, gifts, and insights that come from your journaling process.

Coloring/Writing with Your Nondominant Hand

Coloring and/or writing with your nondominant hand can help you access silent parts of yourself. The emotional part of you that feels deeply is spontaneous, playful, and creative. Trust, appreciate, and celebrate all that comes from inside as you experience using your nondominant hand.

Movement

The movement part of the Integration Reflections invites you to experience yourself more fully. In fostering the connection of the body and other aspects of self, movement is, on some level, your thoughts, feelings, and internal experiences made visible. The invitation to movement is not an invitation to "consciously" move but to be still and listen to yourself from the inside, allowing internal messages or impulses to take the form of physical movement.

Quieting the self allows an open or empty space within. Sit or lie down until something begins to enter the quiet space inside. Feel the change and allow your body to follow where the change leads. *Trying* to move actually stops the movement desired. Learn to let it happen. Movement is to be discovered within, not orchestrated.

When the movement is complete, hold your final body position for a few seconds while you bring your awareness from inside back into the room. Before you move out of this position, make some mental notes on what your physical body is doing. Note your breathing, as well as the position of your arms, legs, and torso. Then gently transition into journaling about your movement experience. Allow your body to return to the last position several times while you complete your journal entry.

Personal Fable Writing

At the conclusion of each segment of the Integration Reflections, there is an invitation to craft a personal fable. The following tips may be helpful:

▸ Review the material you have created, i.e., journal, dream journal, drawing/coloring, movement.

▸ Focus on one or two insights and/or experiences that are most valuable.

▸ Invite your imagination and your child-self to be present.

▸ Allow the material to enter your mind, both as you have written it and from your imagination.

▸ Add any expanded journal entries—drawing, coloring, etc.—to what already exists. Let your imagination create new things, even if they did not occur in your original experience. It is as if you are actually "dreaming" the events at the same time you are making note of them.

▸ Re-write the events in the present tense.

▸ Emphasize the feelings, using feeling words.

▸ Describe the scene and the activity in as much detail as possible.

▸ Describe the characters who are present.

▸ Arrange your material so your story has a beginning, a middle, and an end.

▸ Tell your story out loud to yourself.

▸ Give your story the first title that comes to you.

▸ Tell your story to a friend or group. Include your drawings.

▸ Your fables do not have to be lengthy. Sometimes just a few illustrated paragraphs can capture the essence of your story. Relax and enjoy the process.

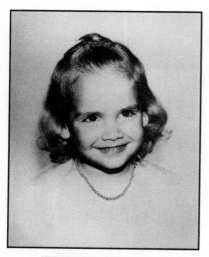

"THERE AND THEN"   "HERE AND NOW"

Charlotte Rogers Brown

Charlotte Rogers Brown lives in Coeur d'Alene, Idaho, with her husband, Charlie. They have three children: Jason, Joe, and Hannah.

With a degree in journalism from Gonzaga University, Charlotte has worked as a news reporter and feature writer for two daily newspapers and a monthly business journal. Her stories have won awards from the Utah-Idaho-Spokane Chapter of the Associated Press and from the Inland Northwest Chapter of the Society of Professional Journalists. A Weaving of Wonder is her first book of fiction.

When she is not at her computer, Charlotte enjoys spending time with her family, reading, hiking in the woods, and taking long walks through her imagination.

Her son Joe once suggested to her that if she were ever asked to compose a page 'About the Author,' she should simply write, "Read my fables."

"THERE AND THEN"

"HERE AND NOW"

Karolyne Smith Rogers, Ph.D.

Karolyne Smith Rogers brings a varied experiential background to her writing. Her life-long belief in the celebration of differences is reflected in her history: public school teacher; coordinator of substance abuse prevention and education programs; director of an outreach program for returning adult students; founding member of The Women's Forum, Inc.; regional and national consultant for Head Start and Hospice; and co-founder of A Center for Human Development, where she currently maintains a private counseling practice.

Her writing includes curriculum design for teacher education, statewide health curricula, a variety of educational training manuals, and numerous original workshops related to life coping skills. She has received the Governor's Award for Creative Excellence for her writing and implementation of substance abuse prevention programs.

Karolyne earned her Ph.D. in adult learning theory from the University of Idaho. She has served as adjunct faculty for the University of Idaho, Washington State University, Boise State University, and Lewis-Clark State College.

Karolyne has a lively sense of humor, is an avid sailor, photographer, native-American flute player, and lover of nature. She enjoys her rural lifestyle in Coeur d'Alene, Idaho.

We are available to groups and organizations
for presentations and workshops.
An audio tape featuring the fables from A *Weaving of Wonder*
and the "Create a Space" script is also available.
For more information, contact:

The Center for Human Development
1802 N. 15th
Coeur d'Alene, ID 83814
(208) 765-9393

Your thoughts about the book are always welcomed and appreciated.
We invite you to write and share your experiences
of A *Weaving of Wonder.*

Charlotte Rogers Brown
Karolyne Smith Rogers

124,